THE PATTERN OF LOVE

The Pattern of Love

BY

WILLIAM P. WYLIE

LONGMANS, GREEN AND CO
LONDON · NEW YORK · TORONTO

LONGMANS, GREEN AND CO LTD
6 & 7 CLIFFORD STREET LONDON WI
THIBAULT HOUSE THIBAULT SQUARE CAPE TOWN
605–611 LONSDALE STREET MELBOURNE C I
LONGMANS, GREEN AND CO INC
55 FIFTH AVENUE NEW YORK 3
LONGMANS, GREEN AND CO
20 CRANFIELD ROAD TORONTO 16
ORIENT LONGMANS PRIVATE LTD
CALCUTTA BOMBAY MADRAS
DELHI HYDERABAD DACCA

First Published 1958

Printed in Great Britain
by Butler & Tanner Ltd
Frome and London

TO

She who walked . . . and walks . . .
like Blanchefleur
'dropping light as all our belovèd do'

CONTENTS

AUTHOR'S NOTE

I MUST thank Dr. Sherwin Bailey and the Rev. E. P. Field, without whose help and encouragement this book would never have been written. I am especially grateful to them for permission to express here certain ideas which were first suggested to me by them. Dr. Bailey in particular has allowed me to put forth, for the first time in book form, his conception of 'acceptable variants' (see Chapter IX). It must be added, however, that neither of these gentlemen should be taken as necessarily agreeing with anything else in this volume.

Very grateful thanks are also due to Mr. Geoffrey Cumberlege and the staff of the Oxford University Press, and to the Rev. Glen Cavaliero, for making available to me the out-of-print volumes of the poetry of the late Charles Williams. Also to Brother George Every, S.S.M., for help and advice.

W. P. W.

ACKNOWLEDGEMENTS

WE are indebted to the following for permission to quote copyright material:

The author's representatives, Messrs. Sidgwick & Jackson Ltd., and Messrs. Dodd, Mead & Company, Inc., for 'Song' from the *Collected Poems of Rupert Brooke* (Copyright 1954 by Edward Marsh); The Oxford University Press for 'Ascension' and 'The Christian Year' from *Poems of Conformity*, and for extracts from *Taliessin Through Logres* and 'On Leaving Church', by Charles Williams; Mrs. Anne Ridler and Messrs. Faber and Faber Ltd. for extracts from *The Nine Bright Shiners*; and Mrs. W. B. Yeats for 'The Song of Wandering Aengus' from *Collected Poems of W. B. Yeats*, published by Messrs. Macmillan & Co. Ltd.

THE SONG OF WANDERING AENGUS

I WENT out to the hazel wood,
Because a fire was in my head,
And cut and peeled a hazel wand
And hooked a berry to a thread;
And when white moths were on the wing,
And moth-like stars were flickering out,
I dropped the berry in a stream
And caught a little silver trout.

When I had laid it on the floor
I went to blow the fire a-flame,
But something rustled on the floor,
And someone called me by my name;
It had become a glimmering girl
With apple-blossom in her hair
Who called me by my name and ran
And faded through the brightening air.

Though I am old with wandering
Through hollow lands and hilly lands,
I will find out where she has gone,
And kiss her lips and take her hands;
And walk among long dappled grass,
And pluck till time and times are done
The silver apples of the moon,
The golden apples of the sun.

WILLIAM BUTLER YEATS. *Later Poems.*

I

CONFUSION WORSE CONFOUNDED

'MARRIAGE BREAKDOWN'; one of the commonest titles for sermons, articles in the serious reviews, conferences, and so forth. Traditional marriage, as it has been understood and practised in the past, does seem, at any rate on the surface, to be breaking down. It might be, however, a truer estimate of the situation to say rather that marriage is in a state of transition; if the suggestion which we shall make is true, namely that something larger and deeper than the hitherto held conventional idea of marriage is emerging from the present chaos, then indeed transition is the right word.

But ages of transition are inevitably ages of confusion, and in this confusion the common man and woman, the ordinary day-to-day lover or spouse, is caught up in a whirl of misunderstandings. The first of these is a failure to recognise the existing divergence between the civil and the ecclesiastical laws of marriage; a divergence which, in a country where the Church is 'established', appears illogical and causes resentment. This divergence has of course been brought into prominence by the controversies over the possible weddings of important persons which were complicated by previous divorce proceedings. It is now realised by most people that this divergence exists, however unpalatable it be. What is not realised is that this divergence is merely a symptom, a severely practical result, of a very much deeper and more fundamental cleavage. A veritable chasm now separates what the traditional Churches seek to teach on the one hand from what, on the other, the ordinary man and woman accept as reasonable and decent standards of behaviour for modern society. It is the difference between religious and conventional *opinion* that worries so many. Leave the law to the lawyers, civil or ecclesiastical: what troubles the ordinary person is something that is at once both vaguer and deeper. And also much more personal, for it affects our most intimate life.

This debate between religious and conventional opinion must be looked into before we can see where we are. Let us take, to represent one side in the controversy, that allegorical figure whom C. S. Lewis introduced to his readers in *Pilgrim's Regress*, and so aptly named 'Mother Kirk'. Mother Kirk, though hard to define, is yet perfectly easily recognised; on this question of marriage she stands for all those institutional Christian bodies and individual persons who adhere to the traditional doctrine of marriage as handed down by the Western Church. Mother Kirk then will include the Roman Catholic Church; she will include the Anglican Church, in so far at least as it remains faithful to its own official formularies; she will include some other organised bodies of Christians; and of course she will include also a countless number of individual persons who still hold to the traditional view. Whenever, then, from this point on, we talk of either Mother Kirk or 'the Church', it is this conglomerate, diffuse, yet nevertheless solidly existent body that we shall mean, a body that believes, in the traditional formula, that 'a validly contracted and consummated marriage no power on earth can dissolve'.

That the number of convinced and practising members of Mother Kirk in this or any other modern secularised state is small, often no more than a tiny minority, may be true enough. Yet there remains a considerable number of people who are willing to pay some respect, even if rather sneaking and shamefaced, to anything which Mother Kirk says. They feel that, after all her long experience, she ought to know what she is talking about; and that therefore to go against her opinions on a matter such as this is something which ought to be done, if at all, only for very grave reasons.

But if we are to face the facts we must also admit that modern society in this country—and that means, by and large, the average man and woman of goodwill and decent principles—just cannot and will not any longer follow Mother Kirk when she states that marriage is, of its very nature, unbreakable. Almost all modern writing, almost every public platform (except partially the pulpit), almost every organ of public opinion proclaims the fact that society not only condones divorce and re-marriage but thoroughly approves of it. It is now considered to be a normal and necessary part of modern life. During a controversy in the national Press about a possible royal marriage, in which one of the parties involved had been previously divorced, it was plainly stated that 'public opinion has given them the all-clear'. So far as the large majority of people in this country was concerned, this statement was accurate; the vast mass of people saw no reason at all why such a marriage should not take place with everyone's full approval. If we stop to consider what is written in books, plays and newspapers, and talked about on the wireless (in addition of course to the actions of a great many people who are considered, and rightly so, as eminently worthy of respect), we must agree that marriage in this country is no longer regarded as being by its very nature unbreakable. Very little social stigma attaches any longer to divorce and re-marriage; and since social stigma tends to-day to be the only criterion of right and wrong, then divorce and re-marriage are considered as perfectly right and proper. Indeed, the boot is really on the other foot now, for it is the refusal to grant a divorce when it is asked for that is considered to be 'wrong' to-day. Fifty years ago if a huddle of suburban housewives were found shaking their heads with disapproval over the conduct of a neighbour, it might very well be because she was so 'wicked' as to be seeking a divorce. But to-day the head-shakings and the lip-pursings would be because she was being so selfish as to refuse the divorce which her husband was demanding. Her attitude would be described as that of the dog in the manger and it would be said that she was wickedly 'denying him his right to happiness'. So far have we moved in half a century.

But the baffling complication of these days arises from the fact that so many of these same people would consider themselves to be attached to, if not practising members of, one or other of Mother Kirk's traditional bodies; especially, in this country of course, the Church of England. There are a large number of persons of real goodwill and honourable intention who will be willing to take their religious opinions—more or less—from traditional Christianity. Such people will however very frequently take their opinions on such subjects as marriage and divorce from the general practice and the accepted conventions of the society in which they live: especially as these are reflected, or even distorted, in the daily Press. This they will do with no sense whatever of inconsistency, for they fail to see that, in this matter at least, religion and social convention proceed from different premises. No wonder then that it is now the Church, now Society, which is attacked; no wonder there is confusion; no wonder that the whole question of marriage is thrown into the melting-pot.

Most of this is of course by now common knowledge; serious-minded people are both aware of it and troubled by it. What they are possibly not quite so aware of is the very complicated chain of historical causes which have brought the present situation into being. It will be part of our task to enquire into these causes, for without such an enquiry progress in any direction will be impossible. But it might perhaps be more profitable for a start to put two questions, which few people seem even to have asked, much less attempted to answer. Perhaps this is because everyone has assumed that the answers were plain; they have, as it were, been taken for granted. But this can no longer be done, and there is no hope at all of letting any daylight into this complicated and obscure situation until both of these questions have been frankly asked, and at least some attempt at an answer has been made.

The first question is one which the Church may quite fairly put to the modern world, remembering that it was after all the Christian Church which gave the institution of marriage as we know it to our Western European civilisation. Moralists, or psychologists such as Oswald Schwarz, may talk about monogamy being natural to human nature, of its being a 'biological fact';[1] anthropologists may talk of the probable evolution of primitive monogamy into polygamy and then back again to monogamy in all the higher cultures; but the plain fact remains that marriage, as our Western world understands it, is Christian marriage. To be more strictly accurate perhaps we should say that marriage in our culture is always either Christian marriage or a development out of—some would say, a degeneration from—Christian marriage. We tend to forget the nature and immensity of the social revolution which the acceptance of the Christian religion by the Roman Empire involved; and nowhere perhaps was it more effective than here. The loose morals of the later Empire have long been a byword; but even Judaism in the time of Christ was often extremely lax in practice. With the establishment of Christianity all this was changed; at least over the

[1] Schwarz, *The Psychology of Sex* (Penguin edition).

institution and stability of marriage there was a fundamental social revolution. It is perfectly true that the
revolution in private morals and manners took very
much longer; but we can truly say that from the time
of the official establishment of Christianity onwards
European man became monogamous in the traditional
sense. That is, he accepted permanent and indissoluble marriage as the pattern of society; it became
the solid institution into which he endeavoured to fit
his personal life. There were perhaps 'safety-valves' to
be found in the intricacies of Nullity and the degrees of
kinship, physical and spiritual; there were winked-at
evasions and personal immoralities; yet the pattern of
life was solidly based on marriage, and marriage itself
was regarded as permanent and unbreakable.

This pattern endured for fourteen hundred years
almost without question. Only in this century has
there been a revolt against it in large areas of our
culture. Nevertheless the revolt has come, and the
pattern is now visibly dissolving before our eyes.

It is for this reason that Mother Kirk has the right
to put her question to the modern world: 'Since you
have abandoned my doctrine of permanent marriage,
what are you going to put in its place?' Or perhaps
more simply: 'Where, and on what principles, are you
going to draw the line?' For society, though it may
have revolted from permanent marriage, is as yet very
far from having decided just what kind of marriage is
to take its place. Consider the state of general public
opinion in Great Britain in the matter of divorce and
re-marriage. One such divorce and re-marriage is
considered to be more or less normal, to be indeed for

many people almost a necessity. Two divorces, however, might cause comment, while three or more re-marriages would be considered to be verging on the immoral. (There is a curious parallel here to what one is told of social convention inside the Soviet Union, as described by Canon Mervyn Stockwood in his book *I went to Moscow*.) One may well ask why there is this tacit disapproval of more than one divorce and re-marriage. On what principle of logic, on what, as yet non-existent, principle of 'semi-permanence' is the line to be drawn at one, or even at two? For if marriage be not permanent of its own nature, then five or six divorces and re-marriages are as justifiable as one. They may prove vastly more expensive; they may cause far more heart-break and sorrow, as they will certainly witness to a high degree of immaturity and irresponsibility; but no logical matter of principle seems to be anywhere involved.

Some would suggest that in putting this question Mother Kirk is playing a trump card; that it is really up to the modern world to prove that its semi-permanent marriage is productive of as much happiness and stability, both for individuals and for society, as was the old tradition of permanence. Dr. Gilbert Russell speaks as a Christian priest, but many will agree with him when he says: '. . . if "happiness" is the touchstone, a society without divorce, though where many husbands took mistresses and many wives lovers, would be happier than our own.'[1]

But this is only one side in the debate, and modern society can well come back with another, equally

[1] *Men and Women*, pp. III, II2.

penetrating, question. Since it was the world which was taught the institution of marriage by the Church, the world which was cajoled, bribed or bullied into accepting permanent marriage, the world has surely the right to an immediate riposte: 'Very well; you taught us marriage. But there is something else which you scarcely ever mentioned; the thing for the sake of which we are now abandoning the strait-jacket of permanent marriage. We have discovered Romantic Love.'

When, in the controversy already referred to, a Press article said 'public opinion has given them the all-clear', one widely circulated newspaper article went on: 'Why not? They love each other.' Disregarding the accuracy or otherwise of such a statement in this or any other particular case, the implication is obvious. Only love counts, and nothing else at all matters. Thus the world may well say to the Church: 'We have discovered something about which you never told us. Insist if you will upon your indissoluble marriage, but tell us first what is the place of romantic love in this institution of yours. Is it an essential and necessary part of marriage? If so, do you mean love before marriage, or after marriage, or both?' It is just here, as we shall see in the next two chapters, that the Church has been caught so badly napping. For far too long the ecclesiastical attitude towards marriage was a sort of 'take-it-or-leave-it'. It was the Church which taught the world marriage, but it would seem that far too often she was merely throwing it to the world in the same way as one throws a bone to a dog, to keep it quiet. There was in some ages a thinly veiled contempt in the average theologian's attitude towards the holy estate of matrimony. Whether or not it was in violent reaction against this, the fact remains that the modern world has discovered romantic love. It knows now, out of the heart of its own experience, that love is something which no one can dare to ignore. Oceans of silly sentiment have been poured out around the name of love, but none of this can alter for one moment the incontrovertible fact that romantic love is an experience which is possible for anyone, vital for many, and which for some people remains the one critical and enduring thing in the whole of life. Love indeed is coming, as we shall see, to take that supreme place in society which, in the 'ages of faith', was reserved for religion. Very naturally Mother Kirk will condemn any such suggestion or practice. But let her beware of doing no more than condemn; let her ask instead whether after all the world may not have discovered something of infinite value. For when the world refuses any longer to deny the power of romantic love, or to pretend that it is not there, the world is surely right.

Now once we have formulated these two radical questions we can begin to see their importance. For they are much more than mere trump cards in the hands of two antagonists looking for debating-points against each other: they are vital factors in human life, in the lives of individuals, and, through them, in the life of society.

Unasked, because we assumed somehow that we knew the answers, these questions are now seen to expose the root problems that lie at the heart of the whole matter. Why is marriage indissoluble? What is the real meaning and nature of that thing which we all know as romantic love? From the moment that either the Church or the world becomes aware of these questions, there will be little comfort and little rest until answers of some kind are found. It will be our principal task, after going into some of the main historical causes that lie behind the present situation and have given rise to it, to attempt at least some sort of answer to the second question. And it may well be that, in examining that question, we may find a rather unexpected answer to the first one as well.

However that may be, we may venture into the field of prophecy for a moment and ask what might be the probable results of satisfactory answers being found to these two questions. Suppose for instance that modern society found that there was after all much more to be said for a permanent and unbreakable union than it had hitherto supposed; that permanence and exclusiveness were demands of the human spirit itself? It would certainly then have to rate marriage a good deal higher than many conventional circles are willing to rate it to-day.

Suppose on the other hand that the Church discovered that romantic love was not only one of the ineradicable potentialities of human nature, but was also in fact a thing of divine origin? Then indeed Mother Kirk would have to take a great deal more notice of romantic love than she has ever done in the past, or than she does even to-day in wide circles of her preaching and thinking.

What would happen, we may well ask, if the Church

was really willing to learn from the revolt against marriage? What would happen if the world were willing
to learn from the dangers that seem quite inseparable
from that revolt? Might not a totally new synthesis
begin to emerge? Might there not arise a pattern of
marriage that would be unlike either the mediaeval
pattern or the modern, but which could yet contain the
values of both? Each of these patterns can so easily
be stigmatised. 'Chattel-slavery!' on the one hand;
'licensed promiscuity!' on the other: these are the cries
which the protagonists hurl at each other. The bad
side of each may well merit such charges. But that
is looking only at the bad side. Are there not positive
values to be found in both, values which neither party,
neither the world nor the Church, can afford to lose?
Can we not hope for a synthesis which might combine the best that is to be found both in human
nature and in divine command?

II

WHEN MOTHER KIRK
WAS AFRAID

We have now to consider how this situation, in which
we are all equally caught up, actually arose. It is easy
enough to say that it was probably due to mistakes
and misunderstandings; but we cannot have much
hope of putting things right unless we can see fairly
clearly just where and how they went wrong. And the
causes lie far back in history. We cannot of course put
back the clock—so we are told *ad nauseam*, and it
happens to be true. Certainly we can never retrace
the roads of history; we can never actually set out
again from any point of wrong departure. But if we
can see where it was and why it was that the right road
was lost, then there might be some hope of regaining
that road; certainly at a point further on, and probably at a much more hopeful and fruitful point. But
in order to be able to do this we must make some real
investigation as to how or where either the Church or
the world, or more probably both of them, wandered
away from the road of certainty and truth.

Let us begin then with Mother Kirk, or more simply
the Church, and look briefly at the record of her

teaching and preaching about marriage and sex: and indeed about love, if we can find any such teaching. We shall probably find that we can distinguish three matters upon which there seems to have been what can only be called a false emphasis. False emphasis is not the same as formal error, but it can, if sufficiently prolonged, lead to a bias that will drive the unwary right off the true path.

The first matter is that of marriage and of the sexual activity bound up with marriage. It would seem that from the earliest times, and right through the greater part of her history, Mother Kirk's attitude towards the sexual side of marriage has been curiously equivocal. There is a strange confusion, a double strand of thought, almost a contradiction, which has never been satisfactorily resolved. G. K. Chesterton, in his great defence of that humanism which is an enduring feature of the continuing orthodox Church as against the Sects, said that many a desert ascetic must have felt in his bones that marriage was a sin. But, he pointedly added, whatever such an ascetic may have felt in his own starved bones, he could never formally teach or preach such a doctrine, because he happened also to be a member of a Church which had already said quite firmly that marriage was a sacrament. This sacramental view of marriage, inherent in the Christian tradition at least from the time of St. Paul, has always been taught by the Church, even in her most rigorist periods. So also has been taught the fact that marriage without sexual consummation lacks its real essence. To this very day in the Roman Church an unconsummated marriage can be dissolved by Papal dispensation. And this is precisely because the natural act which is an essential part of the sacrament has not been performed.

Yet alongside this we have to put at least two other factors. The first is the almost superstitious halo with which virginity was so long surrounded. To-day most Christians would praise virginity, when deliberately chosen, as a consecration and surrender of a particular kind, an offering of the totality of life to the service and glory of God in a special way. As such it is indeed worthy of the highest praise. But the earlier centuries of Christian thought seemed to value virginity far more for the physical fact than for that consecration of the will which we would stress. For them it would almost seem that the mere fact of being untouched by sexual experience was valued more than the offering of the life to God. In a word, the thing which to them was especially praiseworthy was the absence of sexual activity rather than the presence of a surrendered will.

Now from praising the absence of sex it is but a short step—and a fatally easy one for a certain type of mind that is far too common among ecclesiastics of all Christian bodies—to go on to condemn the presence of sexual activity wherever it may be found. Something of this kind of attitude would seem for many centuries to have coloured the Church's view of sexual relations even within marriage. Dare one suggest that Mother Kirk, for all her motherhood, has never lost a certain air of spinsterishness?

Hence the second factor; the assumption by most of the early theologians that there was something of the nature of 'sin' in the act of sexual intercourse even between lawfully wedded persons. One can see how nearly all the Fathers were quite convinced of this. 'Convinced' is not the right word; rather were they like men who accept something without question, who regard it as axiomatic, and then set out to try and explain it: or explain it away, for it was the act itself that was 'sinful', and not merely the fact that men and women were suspected of wanting to perform it for the wrong reasons. (That certainly may have been all too true; possibly still is.) Somehow the 'sinful' nature of the act had to be explained. It was certainly not considered as guilt-bearing sin needing repentance and absolution; it was just taken for granted that there was in the human nature that performed this act something that was not right. One can read extracts from the early Fathers and see them struggling to get away from an impossible contradiction, to free themselves from the horns of a dilemma. After all, God had commanded mankind to be fruitful and multiply; our Lord had instituted the sacrament of matrimony; and even St. Paul had regarded the fleshly union as of the essence of the sacrament. Yet this very act by which the divine will was performed, by which a mystical union pleasing to God was actually fashioned, was still considered to be somehow 'wrong'. How could such things be? How indeed? Yet that they were so seemed quite axiomatic. At first the 'sin' was placed in the strength of the desire, and so intercourse was said to be excused—but why should something which God had commanded need excuse?—when it was performed for the deliberate procreation of children. Only then.

But further insight into the realities of human nature, and we may hope also into the religion that had sanctified every aspect of that nature, forced an advance on this inadequate view. Fortunately St. Paul himself had spoken strong words about the couples who 'defrauded' each other by abstinence. There was then a 'debt' in marriage, something that one partner 'owed' to the other: there were other ends of marriage besides procreation; and it was seen that if intercourse fulfilled these functions, it must be allowable. By this time the term 'excuse' had been removed, and the 'guilt' of either the natural desire or of the parties themselves had been quietly allowed to disappear.

When we reach the full flower of mediaeval thought in St. Albertus Magnus we find a complete realisation of the good of the human body and of all its functions. Indeed, Albertus distinctly says that before the Fall the pleasures of intercourse would have been infinitely greater because of the perfect sensitivity of the body of Man's innocence. Here indeed is an advance.

Mention of the Fall might remind us that the idea was once quite widespread that sexual relationship itself was the actual sin which brought about the Fall. Such an idea has long been abandoned by theologians of unquestionable orthodoxy. But the fact that it should have needed specific contradiction is itself a witness to that strange duality of thought which has perpetually troubled the Church on the subject of marriage and sex. Indeed, though officially disposed of, this idea can still be met in the cruder regions both of Protestantism and Catholicism.

St. Thomas Aquinas acquits intercourse, whether

for procreation or for the payment of the marriage 'debt', of any guilt or sin at all. Indeed, if what he says elsewhere about the essential goodness of all created things be applied here, one would have expected him to say straight out that, in proper circumstances and between the right persons, sexual intercourse must be completely pleasing to God. Yet apparently he could not do it. Even he must strive to find somewhere some kind of 'imperfection' in the act which removed from it the fullness of God's approval. He finds this in what he calls the *ligamentum rationis* of orgasm; the fact that the reason is momentarily out of action and physical functions take control.

It is true that St. Thomas had none of our modern knowledge of nervous reflexes and automotive actions; but one would have thought that, to him of all people, anything which worked in the manner which the Creator had intended must be right. So it would be, we may be sure, in any other field of action. But not, apparently, here. He places the imperfection where it will do least harm both theoretically and in practice, but it is instructive to see how even St. Thomas cannot quite escape from that shadow which had dogged ecclesiastical thought on sex for a thousand years. The religion of the Incarnation had almost triumphed; almost, but not quite.

One might hazard a guess that it was this haunting shadow over intercourse even between married persons which was at least one determining factor in driving the world away from the Church. Men felt that on this (as later on the matter of love) Mother Kirk just did not know what she was talking about.

But what is really far more serious is a sort of secondary idea which flowed from this long held assumption: something which may never indeed have been given in formal teaching, but which was implied in a thousand subtle ways in sermons and exhortations. This was the idea that marriage is somehow a condescension, a licence, even a safety-valve. The Book of Common Prayer cannot be acquitted of this when it calls matrimony 'a remedy against sin, and to avoid fornication'. Men, the Church seems to have thought —and she had reasons enough for thinking so—are by nature licentious and lustful. They cannot be wholly cured, so there ought to be some kind of institution within which this unruly part of their nature can at least be controlled and put to good use. Hence marriage. Matrimony has been given us by divine ordinance (some would have said 'permission' or even 'condescension') and therefore the Church hands out marriage to humanity. But she often seems to do so somewhat grudgingly. 'It is better to marry than to burn.' Whatever St. Thomas or St. Albertus Magnus may have said, this was for far too long a point of popular preaching; it ingrained itself into the ecclesiastical mind in a way that made it extremely difficult to remove. Indeed, in some way the situation seems to have got worse rather than better. St. Augustine in the fourth century tells in his *Confessions* that there had been a time when he had considered putting his passions within the bounds of what he calls 'honourable marriage'. One of the deepest religious thinkers of the seventeenth century was Blaise Pascal, a man of stature almost to be compared with St. Augustine, and

a man whose cast of mind was curiously akin to that
of our own restless modern age. But Pascal wrote of
marriage that it was 'the most dangerous and the
lowest of the conditions of life permitted to the Christian'.[1] Just what, one may wonder, would St. Paul
have made of that?

Marriage then, says the Church, is of God; never
could she deny that. Marriage is of God, and it is
indissoluble. If the recorded words of Christ and of
His immediate followers are to carry any weight, then
the Church was bound to teach the permanence of
marriage. By Christians at any rate, that is by her
own faithful followers, marriage must be regarded as
indissoluble; for the permanence of marriage is a part
of the revelation which she believes has been committed to her. It is therefore also a part of the way of
living which is imposed upon Christians. Believing as
she did, she could not teach anything else. But what
actually happened turned out to be something little
short of a disaster. We have spoken already of the
magnitude of the social revolution which the establishment of Christianity involved; a revolution which,
amongst its other effects, gave monogamy to Western
man. But the establishment of Christianity itself was
only the final result of a life-and-death struggle that
had gone on intermittently for three hundred years.
No protagonists can be left unchanged after passing
through such an experience, and, to pursue our
original metaphor a stage further, when the dust of
conflict had dispersed Mother Kirk was discovered not
only to be dressed in semi-imperial robes, but with a

[1] Mesnard, *Pascal: His Life and Works* (Harvill Press), p. 57.

judge's wig firmly embedded in her hair. The Church inherited and took over the whole judicial concept, and often indeed the actual machinery, of Roman law and justice. That this was a historical necessity few would deny, but its results were as momentous as they were, in one field at least, unfortunate. From henceforth the whole business of marriage was viewed by the Church primarily from the legal aspect. The result of all this is that we can still to a certain extent say that when Mother Kirk talks of sex she can talk only of marriage, and when she talks of marriage she can talk only as a lawyer. The whole theory of sex and marriage was, for the next fifteen hundred years after the 'establishment' of Christianity, to be concentrated on one thing only: who is married to whom according to ecclesiastical law? One might almost think that all that Mother Kirk cared about was to get the generality of sensual men and women safely married, and then to see that they stayed put.

It was not of course the idea of indissolubility that was wrong, not even the preaching of indissolubility; what has proved so fatal is this insistence on the *legal* side of marriage as apparently the only thing that matters, the only thing the Church will worry about.

The next fatal emphasis of Mother Kirk is one of which singularly little notice has been taken; and yet it is possibly one of the most determining factors of all in the revolt of the world against the teaching of the Church. This is the widespread idea that sexual sin is the worst, if not indeed the only, sin, and the even more widespread idea that all forms of extra-marital intercourse are equally sinful.

c

As for the first, we have New Testament authority[1] for holding that there are degrees of sin, and there remain always the deep motives of personality to be weighed and considered as well. A very good example of this question of degrees of sin, and how it may completely upset our normal conventional judgements, can be found in a well-known piece of nineteenth-century artistic history, as described by Nerina Shute in her novel *Victorian Love-Story*. Assuming that the authoress is correct in her assessment of the motives at work in the lives and actions of Millais and Rossetti respectively, what do we find?

According to her, Millais, who was sexually continent and faithful to Effie, not only deserted the Pre-Raphaelite conception of art; he did something very much worse. He deliberately painted what he knew would be popular—though it was against all his real convictions as an artist—simply and solely in order to get money and that entry into high society which money and popularity alone would give, when combined, of course, with respectability. From his own point of view he succeeded admirably.

Rossetti on the other hand, unchaste and unfaithful more than once even to Lizzie, remained poor and outcast simply and solely because he remained faithful to his vision of art. He kept his own artistic integrity.

Can one now put it epigrammatically and say that Rossetti, however rebellious and off the rails in his sexual life, always sought Beauty first: that alone was his life motive. But Millais, in spite of his completely moral sexual life, deliberately gave up the quest for

[1] 1 John 5: 16–17.

Beauty. Now for an artist it is this which constitutes the supreme betrayal, and, if it be true, it may be the damnation of Millais. Further, if the search for Beauty be one of the ways of the search for God, if the following and apprehending of Beauty be one way of apprehending God, then even to search for Beauty in the wrong way and through the wrong persons may well be in the end more pleasing to God (and therefore more truly 'religious') than to abandon that quest for purely selfish or material reasons. Neither man can be acquitted of sin, but if it be the real passions of a life that count, then sexual unchastity is, in this case, seen to be almost a side issue.

So much for the idea that 'sins of the flesh' are the worst sins, an idea quite ineradicable from a certain type of religious mind. What of the other, the equating of all forms of extra-marital intercourse as equally sinful? Into this we must go a little more carefully. If the Church is right in saying that it is ultimately the will of God that sex should only be fulfilled within the bounds of matrimony, then it follows at once that any and every sexual act outside marriage is *ipso facto* sinful. Mother Kirk can never go back on that; and indeed no one would wish her to do so, except those with little regard either for social stability or individual happiness. But we have already seen that we have high authority for believing that there are degrees of sin. The fact that every act of extra-marital intercourse is sinful does not at all mean that every such act is equally sinful. For surely it is just here that personalities and personal motives enter in and make all the difference.

Take two occurrences of everyday life, each of which is, alas! only too common. The commercial liaison between a man and a prostitute is a union which in fact vitiates and lowers the personalities of each of them. On the other hand, the act of sexual union between two lovers who are unmarried may nevertheless be an act which, however illicit, has as its prime motive the attempted fulfilment and enrichment of the two personalities striving to fuse into each other and to realise their unity. Both acts may indeed be sinful, but the contrast in personal feeling, in personal dealing, and in real motive may be almost infinite.

Now the first people to see such a contrast ought to have been precisely those persons whose concern it is to recognise the value of personality, and also to proclaim all the modes and ways of the approach to the vision of Beauty and of God: in other words, the guardians of the religion of the Incarnation. In fact, these have usually been the last to see the difference. How those terrible words 'unclean' and 'impure' have been allowed to befog the picture! One is reminded of the heartfelt cry of Eric Gill in his *Autobiography*, where he tells of the torment and confusion of mind into which he was thrown as an adolescent when he heard what was obviously glorious and wonderful spoken of as if it were unmentionable.

The fact is that the world, out of its own experience, that is the experience of men and women passionately in love and often enriched and ennobled by it, knows perfectly well that all acts of extra-marital intercourse are not equally sinful and ought not to be labelled as such. And when the world, knowing this, sees that all that Mother Kirk seems able to do in any instance is to pass by on the other side, then the world just turns away from her. Regretfully perhaps, but very understandably, it says that she does not know what she is doing. The world knows in its heart, even if it does not always follow it out in practice, that there is indeed a difference between sex and love, allied though they may be. But the Church has for too long refused to recognise any difference; and that is the root of this particular trouble.

The greatest trouble of all, however, is the fact that the Church has almost completely ignored romantic love; that love in whose name the modern revolt against marriage is made. For this Mother Kirk is scarcely to be blamed, at least in the first half of her existence. As C. S. Lewis says,[1] St. Thomas Aquinas does not deal with romantic love any more than he deals with the steam-engine; for the very good reason that he had never heard of either. Into the rise of this conception of romantic love we shall go in the next chapter, but it is a little hard and unfair to blame the Church for ignoring for twelve hundred years something which was equally ignored by the secular society of the time. Since then the situation has changed, but gradually and in a sense almost imperceptibly. Unfortunately the Church's reaction to this change has been almost the same as her reaction over sex. It is a reaction of fear; for the plain truth is that Mother Kirk is afraid. What she fears is sin, and she does well to fear it. One may be permitted to suggest also that she knows a great deal more about sin and about the

[1] *The Allegory of Love*, p. 17.

subtlety with which it works than the modern world does. (Or than it did until the mid-twentieth century showed us the deeds of which so-called civilised man is capable when he thinks they are necessary.) The Church is afraid of sin, and it is just because both sex and love can so easily lead to sin that she seems to fear them. But the same could be said of a great many other things. Nevertheless the fact remains that she has persistently turned her face away from romantic love, and in so doing has ignored the complete revolution in social thought and habit that has been going on around her.

It may startle some people to be told that a religion, whose chief tenet is that God is Love, should be accused of ignoring love. But this is due to a confusion of language, and to some extent also to a confusion of ideas. The fact that most modern translations of the New Testament translate 'charity' in St. Paul's famous eulogy of 1 Corinthians 13 by the word 'love', makes the passage in some sense more intelligible, but also adds to the confusion. We ought to know by now that the early Christians were almost forced to coin a new word to describe that supernatural and burning goodwill to men and women that comes from the Grace of that God Who is Himself all Love. *Agape* in Greek, *caritas* in Latin: this is the word which the Authorised Version of the Bible and the Book of Common Prayer translate as 'charity'. It is a goodwill that behaves to all men—friends, enemies and strangers—in the same way that we behave to those whom we passionately 'love' in the ordinary sense. It is a complete self-surrender to them, as God had given

Himself in the same way for all men. But this is not, emphatically not, what we mean when we talk of romantic love between the sexes.

Yet the matter is not quite so simple as all that; for though the two things may be different, yet there is a connection. How many sermons have been preached, at weddings and elsewhere, designed to shew that 1 Corinthians 13 is a perfect description of the kind of love that exists between two happily married people! On one plane at least it certainly is. But persons who are happily married are, in our modern Western culture at any rate, extremely likely to be persons between whom there has been in the past precisely that thing which we call romantic love. Not only in the past; there is a real sense in which they may be said to have it still. What then is the connection? What have these two kinds of love in common? How are they to be related to each other? Ask Mother Kirk, and we find that so far she has kept her mouth tight shut on the subject.

But this gloomy picture, while accurate enough in its main thesis, is fortunately not the whole story; there have in fact always been traces of a different tradition. While we shall say that on the whole ancient literature, both sacred and secular alike, knows little or nothing of romantic love, yet the Bible does provide at least two exceptions. There is always Jacob who worked seven years for his Rachel, through love of whom they seemed but seven days. It is a solitary reference certainly, but the fact that it is there at all is a proof that the Bible does know all the secrets of the human heart.

If 'Stay me with flagons, comfort me with apples, for
I am sick of love', sounds more Elizabethan than
Biblical, being in fact both, we can never get away
from 'My beloved is mine and I am his: he feedeth
among the lilies'. Both these quotations are from the
Song of Solomon, as it is called in the Authorised Version. It must confirm one's faith in the guidance of
the Holy Spirit that both this book and *Ecclesiastes*
ever found their way into the Canon of sacred Scripture—and still more that they have stayed there.
There they are, ready to be a standing rebuke to
Christians if ever they shy away from love. But it is
instructive to see what has happened to these passages. The good divines who made the headings for
the more usual editions of the Authorised Version,
following the traditions of the 'Catholic fathers and
ancient bishops', just could not imagine that such
words, in their literal meaning, had anything at all to
do with religion. They could not possibly, so they
thought, mean what they said; they must mean something else. And so they are said to be an expression of
'The mutual love of Christ and His Church'. Doubtless they can be taken as this; and Christian devotion
has surely not been wrong in ascribing this meaning
to them, and in meditating devoutly on these lines.
All this, we may say, they also are. But the importance
lies in the word 'also'; they have a literal meaning and
a literal message.

Yet maybe these divines were wiser than they knew.
The Church has always been saved by a small rem-
nant, and while Mother Kirk has on the whole turned
her eyes away from romantic love with considerable

resolution, there were always some few who had a wisdom of a different kind. It began perhaps with that early saint, Ignatius of Antioch, who on his way to martyrdom so startlingly exclaimed 'My Eros is crucified!' And it continued amongst those who might perhaps have been least expected to have any sympathy at all with romantic love. Or perhaps not; for genuine saints, and especially the mystics, do know the human heart better than anyone else.

Now when these saints and mystics looked around for a picture by which they could attempt to describe that ecstatic union between the soul and God that was their own special experience, they could in the end find no other description than that of what we are calling romantic love. That is why, when they turned to the Bible, they chose just those portions of Holy Scripture which the ecclesiastics were busily engaged in explaining away. They did not do that; for they realised that no other picture could explain what they were after. And, even if they never actually said so, they must surely be taken to imply that the picture itself came from God.

We can say of course that it was St. Paul himself who began the process when he talked of the mystery of marriage and likened it to the mystical union between Christ and the Church. Both were mysteries, and both were 'one-flesh' mysteries, and the connection was plain. But Paul was talking of institutions; therefore he talked of marriage. The mystics were talking of the individual; and they talked of love.

Somewhere within the Church, we may then say, there has always lain the knowledge of what romantic love really is. But it has been hidden and allowed to get overgrown. May it not perhaps be that this present age, in which the Church is confronted with a revolt against her marriage doctrine, is precisely the age in which God is calling her to dig out and recover her hidden doctrine of love? May not the present confusion be in fact her opportunity?

III

WHERE THE WORLD
WENT WRONG

IF the Church may be said to have ignored or despised the phenomenon of love, the world has certainly taken an opposite course. Whether or not by a sort of automatic reaction, the world has run after love to such an extent that it is at least in grave danger of losing the right road.

It might be more accurate however to say that this is what the world has been doing ever since the day when Western Man first awoke to the fact of love's existence; for this whole business of the centralisation of personal emotion and social habit around what we call 'falling in love' is a comparatively modern idea.

This being so, we ought in all fairness to remember that the Church's system of ethics and morality was largely formulated in ages to which romantic love was a stranger. And we know only too well how, in ecclesiastical circles at any rate, that which has already been formulated tends to become more and more fixed and rigid as time passes.

It was probably C. S. Lewis in his fascinating book

The Allegory of Love who first propounded the theory that love was a modern discovery. The book is primarily a study of a certain phase of European literature; the mediaeval and late-mediaeval. Some people therefore might be tempted to dismiss it as having little or no connection with everyday life. They would be wise to resist the temptation, and to listen to what Professor Lewis has to say of the origin of that force which now rules everyday life more powerfully perhaps than anything else. It is true of course that his thesis has not been allowed to go unchallenged. We have no competence to pass any judgement upon the literary questions involved, but we must say that if what he suggests is really true, then indeed it is a matter of vastly greater importance than mere belles-lettres, or the interpretation of mediaeval manuscripts. He is delving deep into our whole manner of social thought and practice.

Now whatever criticisms may be passed on his thesis as a whole, the following passage would seem quite incontrovertible to anyone who has even a nodding acquaintance with the classics:

> It seems to us natural that love should be the commonest theme of serious imaginative literature; but a glance at classical antiquity or at the Dark Ages at once shows us that what we took for 'nature' is really a special state of affairs, which will probably have an end, and which certainly had a beginning in eleventh-century Provence. It seems . . . or it seemed to us till lately . . . a natural thing that love (under certain conditions) should be regarded as a noble and ennobling passion: it is only if we imagine ourselves trying to explain this doctrine to

Aristotle, Virgil, St. Paul or the author of *Beowulf* that we become aware how far from natural it is.[1]

Most people might perhaps be prepared to accept St. Paul as being ignorant of love—though one may well ask why—but the thing that really startles in this passage is the introduction of pagan and classical names. It is only when we realise that the greatest poet and the greatest philosopher of antiquity are alike assumed to be unaware of the very existence of romantic love, that we realise something of the magnitude of this revolution which began in the eleventh century. Elsewhere C. S. Lewis calls it one of the half-dozen really fundamental changes that have ever befallen the human spirit.[2]

Whether or not it was the troubadours of Provence who were responsible, it does seem that something then happened which initiated a change in fundamental thought about the man-woman relationship; and from change in thought began change also in social custom and practice. Something had suddenly appeared from almost nowhere, something that from now on was to be written about, talked about and thought about; and it was largely something which neither pagan nor Christian had thought about before. As Dr. Lewis emphasises in another passage, its appearance and general acceptance by our society has 'erected impassable barriers between us and the classical past or the Oriental present'.[3]

All this seems to be quite undeniable; and then we

---

[1] *The Allegory of Love*, p. 3. [2] Id., p. 11.
[3] Id., p. 4.

have to remember that the Church was born and matured in that classical past that knew not love, that it was in that period that her outward characteristics and ways of thought were moulded. And then a whole new world of thought and feeling began to grow up and spread abroad, and, though that new world is now itself some seven centuries old, yet Mother Kirk has never quite been able to make herself at home in it.

Something, we say, happened; but what? Romantic love, we suggested, was 'discovered', but that cannot be quite true for there is a sense in which love was always there. To some extent at any rate men and women must always have loved, just as they have always married, and always lusted too. 'Noticed' would perhaps be a safer word to use than 'discovered'; for up to this time love had always been a purely private matter, an odd sort of affair that blew up between certain people—perhaps odd people too. Even though there might be many more of these than was generally suspected, little or no notice of the thing was taken by society as a whole; it was not something that came into the general scheme of life. It wasn't talked about and sung about; and, above all, life was not arranged around it, in the sense in which almost everything to-day is arranged around love. It did not, or it was not at any rate supposed to, affect the motives and the lives of the participants in the way in which it is now alleged to. Love, while it must have existed long before even Jacob loved Rachel, had so far been completely ignored in general thought and social fashion. No one ever considered that it was a motive for arranging lives, scarcely even for doing anything out of the ordinary; it just was not in any sense at all either a convention of society or an expected part of ordinary life.

It was this that the troubadours altered, for it was probably they who plucked love out of the obscurity in which it had lain hidden from time immemorial. And, having done this with a flourish of trumpets, they then set love high on a pedestal and invited the world to come and worship at the shrine of their new-found goddess. There will always be dispute as to the exact sense which we are to ascribe to the word 'love' as they used it. *Amour courtois* was a new thing, and, like all new things, was capable of development; and development can always be in either of two directions, a higher or a lower. To say that our modern conception of an ennobling and enduring passion that fulfils the whole life and character of the lovers is one development, must be paralleled by saying that the sloppy sentimental nonsense of the dance-hall and the cinema is the other. Neither may be quite like the original. Yet both have undeniably descended from it, for we may take it as reasonably certain that something, some recognisable experience at least akin to what we describe as 'falling in love', did burst suddenly upon the notice of the literary general public at some time in the eleventh century. *And it has gone on growing steadily both in notice and in importance ever since.* If Mother Kirk's false emphases go back to the Middle Ages, the world's reactions go back equally far; we have to dig very deep to find the roots of our present-day confusions and misunderstandings.

Now it is very important to remember that this so-called discovery of romantic love took place in a society in which there was already the fixed social pattern of indissoluble marriage. For seven hundred years and more this had been the pattern; a pattern into which individuals were not only ordered to put their lives, but were, from age-long habit, accustomed to doing so. And like all social institutions, marriage had tended to become something purely conventional; when, indeed, not frankly utilitarian. Therefore, as C. S. Lewis forcibly reminds us, the first effect of any doctrine of romantic love in a society that is based on the conventional institution of marriage, cannot be anything but adulterous. Marriage is the institution, and marriage, in a society where love is unacknowledged, cannot have any connection with love (that is, in social thought, whatever individual persons may have thought or felt privately). It follows that any kind of love which is either brought actually into being, or which is suggested as being a thing worth seeking, must be love outside and apart from marriage. That is, it must be adulterous.

Nothing else could have been expected from such a new and disturbing phenomenon, and it is exactly what happened. The Courts of Love, with all their elaborate codes and etiquette of chivalrous behaviour, always thought and spoke of love as a thing completely apart from marriage. The two were not considered as having anything at all to do with each other. They were not allowed in fact to have any connection, for the lady whom the lover worshipped from afar—or even from not so far—just could not be

his wife: not even his possible wife, for there was a
sense in which courtly love actually forbade marriage.
'Any idealisation of sexual love, in a society where
marriage is purely utilitarian, must begin by being
an idealisation of adultery.' [1] It need not of course
end like this; it need not even stay like this, but the
chances are that the damage will already have been
done. The terrible, but quite inevitable, result will be
that the Church will mistrust the idea of love from the
very start. How could it be otherwise? This new conception lauded to the skies something which she considered, and rightly considered, to be a mortal sin.
How could Mother Kirk, at that time, do anything
else but turn away?

It might also be conceded that those glorious
mediaeval stories of the great lovers (what we might
call the holy scriptures of the new religion), the stories
of Tristram and Iseult, of Lancelot and Guinevere,
of Troilus and Cressida, can have done little to
assuage the theologians' very natural fears. If love
was always going to end in tragedies like these, then the
sooner weak and erring mortals ceased to think about
it the better. We may at least give the Church the
credit for having really tried to keep men and women
out of danger; and not only out of danger of damnation through sin, but also out of danger of the frustration, the heart-break and the tragedy which this
kind of affair so often seems to bring. Love has its
disasters as well as its triumphs.

It is true of course that the situation gradually
changed. But it is also to be feared that, as in the

[1] *The Allegory of Love,* p. 13.

D

allied matter of sex, Mother Kirk never really got over the shock to her sensibilities, and indeed to her respectability, which the first promulgation of romantic love gave her. It ought to be no small part of our present task to help her to see this dangerous phenomenon (and may the world on its side be willing to admit the dangers!) with new and perhaps more sympathetic eyes.

The situation did change, and changed comparatively soon. *Arthurian Torso*, by Charles Williams and C. S. Lewis, tells us that in some of the later Grail poems, such as *Erec* and *Cligès*, romantic love was quite definitely brought into the matter of marriage. The whole of *The Allegory of Love* itself is an attempt to trace the various steps by which the courtly love of the troubadours was gradually brought within the circle of Christian ethos and behaviour, until, by the time we reach Spenser and *The Faerie Queen*, romantic love and marriage have become quite compatible. Dare we say they have almost become bedfellows?

That would have been all right, had only opinion steadied there. But time, alas, does not stand still, and meanwhile further changes in society were coming fast: ominous changes such as would have shocked the troubadours possibly as much as they would have startled Spenser. Two things were to happen before we could reach the mid-twentieth century and our modern world: one of them a long drawn out and very gradual process, the other quite startling in its suddenness. To mention the latter first, a complete and utter change in the status of woman in our modern Western society has resulted from the so-called 'feminist' movement. The 'emancipation of woman' has immeasurably raised her status, and has given her an independence . . . if not always a corresponding dignity . . . unknown alike to the eleventh and to the sixteenth centuries. Woman is now a person in her own right, chattel or slave of none, and she claims an equal right to life, untrammelled by the conventions or the rules of a largely man-made society. The effect of this demand, and of its at least nominal acceptance by society, upon an institution such as marriage, in which woman had hitherto been assumed to be the subordinate partner, has been, and is, quite shattering. That is no real part of our enquiry; but the change has been equally profound in the mental attitude assumed by woman before marriage. Woman will now claim an equal say in the motives for entering into marriage; two full and equal personalities will now have to be taken into account before any marriage is contemplated. And that will mean that in the whole matter of love woman will demand equality. If love is to be accepted as a normal part of life, then into that matter too will have to go all the different ways of thinking that characterise the human female as well as those characteristic of the male. That this leads to many complications is obvious enough.

The other social change to which we referred is the slow but steady growth by which this new discovery of romantic love finally became what it is to-day, a determining part both of social convention and of personal life. It could best be described as the process by which, from the middle of the eleventh century, romantic love has been as it were progressively 'loosed upon the world'. This process has coincided exactly with, as it was largely caused by, another process: that of the cheapening of literature.

As the years went by, literature of all kinds became more readily accessible and more widely diffused; the reading public became steadily wider and wider. The result was that what had started perhaps as a mere literary idea or a group of aristocratic assumptions became, first the ideas, and then the behaviour, not of the favoured few but of the mass of the people. Soon all could know about romantic love, even if only few could sing worthily of it. Now combine this with the raised status of women and the idea soon flowered that love, for both men and women, was something that had an absolute value of its own.

But the word 'cheapening' has unfortunately another meaning. Hand in hand with the wider spread of literature went the vulgarisation of its more popular (and more and more accessible and widely read) portion. This meant that the whole idea of love became gradually clouded over with popular senti-ment. We are apt to smile at some of the sentimental nonsense which the nineteenth century produced. But we have little right to do so, for it is our own century which has gone furthest in the vulgarisation of the ideas of love and romance; and immeasurably further in the spreading of the cheaper ideas at the expense of the more serious ones. Cheap literature exists in plenty, but as the real moulder of public opinion it has been completely eclipsed by the cinema. For fifty years now the floods of sentiment have been poured out, so that every civilised country (and many uncivilised as well) has been swamped and drenched by the sugary concept of love which is dear to the hearts of the film-magnates, as interpreted by the film-stars. The degree to which the whole conception of love will have been lowered and weakened in the process is tragically obvious.

C. S. Lewis suggested that it would have been hard for the troubadours to explain to St. Paul just what they meant by *Amor*. One may suggest that any modern suburban girl would be even harder put to it to explain to any troubadour just what she means by her passionate hope of 'Mr. Right waiting round the corner'.

Yet just because she may be incapable of explaining her dream, we have no right to dismiss that dream as meaningless. Because the troubadours could not explain it to St. Paul, the successors of the Apostles have no right to deny that the troubadours may have stumbled upon one of the fundamental secrets of the human heart. Nor has any of us the right to deny that the little suburbanite may be seeking for something which, in spite of its shoddy clothing, can still be intensely real. No amount of cheapening, or silly sentiment, should blind us to the fact that here we are face to face with one of the root facts of human nature, one of the greatest possibilities open to the heart of any man or woman. If the Church fails to recognise this, then she will be failing the modern world in one of its most pressing problems, for she dare not any longer turn a blind eye to that force of love which is now, for good or ill, the driving force of modern society.

We have now traced the wrong emphasis and changing ideas of both the Church and the world back to at

least the eleventh century; but since that time something else has been happening which has had a most
profound effect upon the mental atmosphere of our
modern world. It was once called by a broadcast
speaker 'the death of God'; and it is in fact a pro-
gressive fading out of any active belief in God. It is
true that the troubadours may have had little enough
conscious thought of God, and still less respect for His
commandment against adultery. Nevertheless, belief
in God was a paramount factor in the mental atmosphere of their age, in a sense which it is certainly not
to-day. The modern world goes its way, in the matter
of love as in so many other things, largely bereft of
any consciousness of God at all. Yet when men forget God, or seek to banish Him from their motives,
strange things are apt to happen.

Few people seem to have noticed the very penetrating analysis of modern social and industrial conditions which was put forth, in the first year of the late
war, by Dr. Eric Mascall in his little book *Man: his
Origin and Destiny*.[1] He points out there that mediaeval
men, however selfish and wicked in their actions,
always acknowledged God's supreme importance. The
mental assumptions forming the background of their
society both acknowledged God and assumed the sub-
servience of Man. Therefore the way things were
looked at, the scale of values which was unquestionably accepted, could be described, he says, as a sort
of pyramid of values of descending order: God; Man;
Things; Money. Each of these *existed for* the one
above and served it; and so a just balance was pre-

[1] Dacre Press, 1940.

served. The Renaissance altered all this; for Renaissance man made the deliberate attempt to place Man himself at the top of the pyramid. This meant of course displacing God, but no one thought that this would affect society; the rest would surely stay as it was.

The result of centuries of this process is the age in which we are now living: an age which has produced something that is quite startlingly different from what had been hoped and intended. Man is no longer at the top of the pyramid; the whole thing has got itself reversed and is now standing on its head. For, says Dr. Mascall (and with a good deal of truth, surveying our industrial world as it existed in 1939), the most important thing is now assumed to be Money. That is, prime importance is now given to things like Profits, Credit, Financial Stability, etc. Things exist now only in order to be sold and make money; Men exist primarily in order that they may make things which can be sold for profit; while as for God: if God exists at all He is thought of as being there merely in order to help and comfort men if and when they may happen to want Him. The modern pyramid of importance is: Money; Things; Men; God. And this deplorable state of affairs is entirely due to the removal of God from the top of the scale.

Now whether or not we choose to accept this as an accurate analysis of modern urbanised and mechanised life, it would look as if something rather similar had happened in the matter of romantic love. For the centuries during which romantic love has steadily increased its hold upon the world have also been precisely those centuries during which the idea of God has been progressively fading out of the consciousness of Western Man. There is a sense indeed in which the former has tended to take the place of the latter, the vacuum caused by the removal of God having been at least partially filled by this new concept of love. In reality, something worse than this has happened; for love is regarded, not as 'God', but rather as a sort of blind impersonal fate. 'God', after all, means something personal, some power whom we are free to obey or to disobey; our response can at least be chosen and willed. But no one has any choice at all when they are overtaken by a blind, unseeing fate. And that is precisely what this modern conception of love amounts to. When love strikes we are all helpless in its toils; nothing can be done about it at all.

This muddled kind of thinking which confuses Fate with the desire to follow one's own indulgence, and which tries to cover both of them with a sort of half-memory of the word 'God', is finely illustrated in Shelley Smith's mystery novel *The Woman in the Sea*. Early in that book we have a picture of foolish Zoë Robinson meditating upon her adulterous love, that love which is the eventual cause of the murder and the suicide which make up the plot of the story. Zoë meditates thus:

> But he loved her, and surely something which felt so right could not be wrong . . . and would God have let them love one another if it was wicked? God was not so cruel. He never meant you to be unhappy. . . . Everyone said that. . . . No; it was 'meant' that they should love one another. It was their destiny.

In how many adulterous and illicit love-affairs of real life does one not find the name of God thus brought in as some sort of excuse? But the God Who is thus invoked is not the God Who would be recognised by any Christian, by any theist; it is this new 'love-fate' which is meant. It may be suggested that this idea has now become perhaps the most fatal and pernicious of all the modern heresies. It is probably responsible for breaking up more homes than is any other single factor.

Yet even while we condemn, we must remember that, like all heresies, this idea is only a perversion, or an ill-balanced presentation, of a truth. It is in fact only the modern boiled-down, over-sentimentalised and also over-stressed result of that discovery, or 'notice', of love which occurred originally so long ago. But this was after all only a notice of something which in itself is intensely real. It may well have worked even before it was noticed; but now that it has come out into the light of day its reality and its power must be recognised for what they are. For good or ill we now know something of the power of romantic love over men and women; a power capable of immense good as of immense evil. It is a power, let us remember, that can make at least as often as it can break.

On this discovery we can never go back. We must be careful here. The Church was afraid of love, as she was afraid of sex, and in her fear she ignored it. That was her fatal mistake, to react away in fear instead of drawing near in understanding. But the title of this chapter suggests that the world went wrong too. So it did; but not in discovering love. *That* was not the world's mistake; far from it: for we may later see reason to suggest that this discovery of romantic love in the eleventh century was one of the most important things that ever happened in opening man's heart to God as well as to his fellow men and women. It was not the discovery of love that was wrong, not even the pursuit of love, except when that became unbalanced. No: the wrong turning came in the over-sentimentalising of love, its cheapening, and above all in the putting of love in the place of God, the turning of love into Fate.

The world needs to look back to the origin and real meaning of that love which is now so often both a terror and a torment. The Church needs to look back and face her fear, and so cleanse herself from it. Both need to look back and then, on the basis of what they can discover in a real searching of their own hearts, attempt a new and juster balance for the future.

But the Church will not do this without a good deal of hard thinking; a good deal of probing for fundamentals which have so far either been ignored or, on the other hand, perhaps been taken too easily for granted. And we can begin to see now that the prime questions for the Church could be phrased something like this: What is the real meaning and nature of this love which has been discovered by the world? What has it to do with the God from Whom in the end come all things? What, on the other hand, really is marriage? Why should Christ have pronounced marriage to be indissoluble? Above all, of course, and most important: What is the connection between love and marriage? What ought it to be? And there is a subsidiary question too that cannot be ignored: What is the relation and connection (if any) between the experience of falling in love and what is known as 'religious experience'? But at the heart of any such enquiry there lies the matter of love, for it is after all love which men and women actually experience. And all experience comes, in the last analysis, from God. Men may not always know this; they may even choose to forget it. But Mother Kirk knows it; the question is, does she understand it?

IV

THE NEW LOOK

WE ended a previous chapter with the suggestion that, in spite of all the aberrations which appear so prominent, there has nevertheless lain hidden somewhere within the Church a real knowledge of the nature of love. From the tantalising hints of the Primitive Church ('My Eros is crucified') and down through the mystics, to say nothing of the actual life in grace of millions of devout Christian lovers, there is the continual hint of something waiting to be told. The trouble is that so far no one seems to have tried to tell it clearly and plainly. It is surely the Church's task to-day to turn round and begin to shed some light on places which seem hitherto to have been kept almost deliberately dark. Already there is discernible a somewhat new turn, a 'new look', in theological thinking, and it is to this that we must direct our attention.

The best way to start is by going back to that fundamental factor that lies at the back of all discussion of, or actual practice of, marriage, the factor of sex. It is, after all, only when we have a thorough understanding of sex, of its nature and meaning as well as of its powers and possibilities, that we can hope to have any thorough understanding of love or of marriage. Great though love and marriage may be in their own right, they are yet, on the plane of human nature, only derivatives of sex. So it would appear, at least to a first glance, for later on we may have reason to modify such a statement. But let us start with the simplest of all questions; what is sex for?

Now to that question it would have been thought, until very recently, that there were only two possible answers. The first, and the most obvious on the philosophical plane at any rate, is that sex is for procreation. As someone once put it rather baldly, we are all born with half the machinery for reproduction and with an intense desire to find someone with the other half. The second answer springs directly from this desire, and is an equally obvious answer if one starts from premises somewhat removed from the philosophical. As this is what the majority of men and women do, we may say that their answer would be that sex is for the pleasure of the individual. (That is, they would answer thus if they honestly expressed the motives which drive them.)

Of these two answers Mother Kirk has always approved of the former. Did not the Creator Himself command mankind to be fruitful and multiply? It was part of the tangle into which theological thought had twisted itself that for so many centuries the obeying of this command, or rather the performance of the only act by which it could be obeyed, was nevertheless considered to be 'sin' or at least 'imperfect'. We have seen how this idea just managed to survive the full flower of mediaeval thought, how it rose again in Puritanism and Jansenism, and how it still survives in some ecclesiastical backwaters.

But honesty would compel us to admit that it is the second answer, the almost unconscious assumption of unregenerate human nature, which has always swayed men and women the most. On this the Church would seem to have frowned severely; but her reasons for doing so ought to be looked into a little more closely.

It could scarcely be expected that she would approve of the complete cutting out of procreation. It is true also that Mother Kirk has always nourished in her bosom the type of mind which seems to take delight in condemning anything at all which makes for pleasure. Such minds have flourished in every age, and have all too often come to high office in the Church; presumably, we may hope, for their other virtues. But when this fact is combined with the Church's real knowledge of the many dangers into which sexual and romantic pleasure can undoubtedly lead men and women, then we can see the cause of some of those denunciations whose fierceness was only equalled by their unwisdom. Fortunately there has always been a better balanced Christian tradition; there have always been those who knew that, while pleasure may indeed be dangerous and the pursuit of pleasure for its own sake may be the road to damnation, yet pleasures of any kind can have—indeed ought to have—a perfectly legitimate place in the Christian life. More than that; if they are such as are within the Will and Purpose of God, then their enjoyment itself may be a glorification of God. And of all pleasures, this ought surely to be more possible for sex than for any others, save only eating and drinking.

It is commonly supposed that it is only the aberrations and false emphases which made the Church frown so severely upon this second explanation of the purpose of sex. But it may be that she knows of some purpose of sex other than either procreation or the mere pleasure of the individual. It may be that, apart altogether from the matter of procreation, she has barred the road to merely individual pleasure because she has all along been dimly aware of something infinitely more important. We must not call her obscurantist before we are sure; and some of the new turns in modern theology should make us pause before passing judgement.

'Apart altogether from the matter of procreation' is the key phrase, because that is what has now happened; sex is being thought of, by both the world and the Church, in some sense apart from procreation. There is no need to discuss the social revolution in habit and idea which the extension and perfecting of contraceptive technique has brought about in the last generation or two. Leaving aside for the moment all questions of morals or ethics, it is probably now true to say that in our modern Western world the vast majority of married couples are practising contraception in some form or other. Indeed the use of artificial contraceptives is everywhere being taken for granted (whether rightly or wrongly is not the point for the moment) in the widest circles of our society. The result of all this can only be that people tend more and more to think of sexual intercourse apart from procreation. It is almost as if there were a return to the mentality of those extremely primitive tribes of savages who do not know that there is any connection between sexual intercourse and pregnancy. Coitus and conception are no longer indistinguishable in thought and habit; they have become separate things.

We cannot deny that the Church has followed suit in some degree. It has always been a point of Catholic theology that coitus is not only lawful but part of the 'marriage debt', a thing that ought to be practised by married persons, even when, as in cases of known sterility or after the menopause, it is known that no conception can possibly result. It is surely impossible then for the Church to suggest that it is *exclusively* procreational. But modern Catholic theology has in fact moved a good deal further than this. Artificial contraception may still be condemned by the Roman hierarchy, but it would seem that 'family planning' is regarded as a rational matter. The recommendation by Catholic theologians of the 'rhythm method' or the 'safe period' means that coitus is still approved even when it seems certain—to what degree may probably vary with individuals—that conception will be impossible, or highly unlikely.

On the use of artificial contraceptives Mother Kirk is of course divided. As is well known, it is the practice of the Roman Church to condemn their use; other Christians have different views. It might best be put by saying that all Christians are now agreed that coitus can no longer be regarded as exclusively for procreation, but that it has another quite distinct purpose which it can always fulfil.[1] Where they continue to differ sharply is as to whether or not the use of artificial contraceptives is a wise or a moral method of ensuring this other purpose, should procreation not be desired at the same time. It is in fact one particular method of severing coitus from conception that is condemned by some, not the severance itself. This difference of opinion may be deep, but it is really a small matter compared with the revolutionary change that has come in the finding of, and seeking for, some other purpose in coitus.

This having been said, what is now left? On the old idea of there being only two answers to the purpose of sex, we would now be left with only the pleasure of the individual. That there are many men and women who do not seem able to rise above what may be called the 'entertainment value' of sex is true enough. Yet the world in general has advanced beyond that, for surely all human experience shews that entertainment value, of whatever kind, is at least doubled by being shared. If theory suggests that coitus cannot be exclusively for the purpose of procreation, experience shows that neither can it be exclusively for that of individual pleasure. Is it possible that the world and the Church are at last beginning to approach nearer to each other by way of this new method of apprehending sex and sexual experience? Most people would be inclined to deny this, but a little thought suggests that in fact they are considerably nearer to each other than is commonly supposed. For both are

[1] For further discussion of this point, see my *Human Nature and Christian Marriage* (S.C.M. Press, 1958).

E

now beginning to think, not of the individual, whether it be either of the separate partners, or the new-born result of their co-operation, but of the pair of lovers considered *as a pair*.

Now one of the first things to get quite clear in our minds, even from a purely empirical point of view, is the relationship between sex and love. Though obviously connected in the closest manner, they are manifestly not the same thing; and this in spite of the frantic efforts of hedonistic and sensual men to suggest that they are. That they are not the same is proved by the fact that it is always possible to have the one without the other. A man consorting with a prostitute enjoys sex, but he may have no love for her at all, even of the most trivial kind. Many passionate lovers on the other hand refrain from any sexual expression of their love. But men and women also know that, while each of the two things can be experienced apart from the other, yet each one by itself is woefully incomplete unless it is joined to the other. Even the 'entertainment value' of sex is torn in half if there be no love between the parties. While love without sexual expression, no matter how high may be the motives for abstention, is always frustrated and loses its right fulfilment. Coitus misses not only its full enjoyment, but what men and women instinctively know to be its purpose, when that other union of love is not present. And that union which love both makes and desires can have its full expression only in the sexual action. It is then the union of persons, the joining of the pair into a union greater than themselves, which the world knows ought to be both the purpose and the result of coitus. 'Ought to be' rather than 'is' of course, for so many other factors may enter in, and so many mistakes may be made. And yet even so, something that is sought in the wrong way and according to wrong methods or codes may yet in itself be something that is rightly desirable. It may often be a desire for the right thing that drives men and women, weak both in will and in understanding, to seek it in the wrong way.

Now the new turn, the 'new look', of modern theological thinking not only understands all this, it does much more: it explains it. And it explains it from a theological, and therefore ultimately also from a moral, point of view. When the world comes to understand this, then the world may perhaps be willing to give to us the attention which it was not willing to give to former generations of moral preachers. And the explanation may save the world from running wild after something which, while it is undeniably good, is also explosively dangerous.

We can begin this part of our study by going back to that primal doctrine of the Judaeo-Christian tradition, the doctrine that Man is made in the image of God. This is an axiom of our religion; the teasing question is, in what quality or qualities of men does the image lie? Where is it to be found? This problem of the image of God in Man has troubled the theologians and philosophers for centuries. What is it about Man that is most like God? The answers have been many and various; but there is one that is of very special importance for our subject. God is the Creator, and Man is a creative animal; he makes things, he delights to make things, and 'all their desire is in the work of their craft'.[1] Procreation is then a part of Man's creative activity, for one cannot make things in any more essential and real way than by procreating human beings, by actually reproducing oneself. Man is creative because God is the Creator, and it is in this respect that Man is most truly the image and likeness of God.

That this is no mere theological subtlety, without effect upon daily life, it takes only a little thought to see. Half the trouble with modern industrialism (the problems of automation etc.) and half the frustrations of urban mass-produced life, are the direct result of twisting, denying or crushing this essential creativeness of men and women. Instead of a nation of craftsmen we are now producing a nation of button-pushers and pen-pushers; and then we seem surprised that men and women are angry, frustrated, irresponsible and rebellious. It is more often than not simply the natural result of a life that denies them any real chance of being men—men created in order that they too may create. It is here that a great deal of the sentimental talk about religion being the only solution of industrial troubles entirely misses the mark, because it talks only of better relations between employers and employed. 'A new spirit in industry' would certainly be a good thing, and a Christian thing; but real doctrinal Christianity would surely say that the first and primal thing to do would be to restore to man that which God gave him; his chance of being really creative. All else is no more than palliative.

[1] Ecclesiasticus 38 : 34.

There is a startling remark made by that neglected writer and prophet, the late Arthur Machen. In his delightful novel *The Secret Glory*, he makes an old Welshman say that 'a brothel is a house of sanctity compared with a modern factory'. If it is indeed true that a modern mass-production factory destroys or perverts the creative instinct of man, and in so far as this is true, then this must be a worse sin than something which merely releases immoderately another side of this same instinct. The one liberates the instinct in a wrong way, but the other destroys the instinct altogether, and in doing so takes away from Man the most important thing about him—his likeness to God.

One can see now how this placing of the image of God in the creative instinct is going to cast a shadow of glory over our whole subject. The image of God has been found by some to lie in Man's free will and power of choice; by others in the rational faculty, the intelligence which differentiates Man from the animals; by others again in the moral sense, or in that altruism and capacity for self-sacrifice which mirrors the self-giving of God in the Act of Redemption. Now we may agree that in any or in all of these faculties men and women may be said truly to reflect some aspect of the Divine Nature. All of them may be a part of the image of God.

But there is one thing to note about these theories. However true or suggestive they may be in themselves, every one of them is limited to the individual man or woman. It was to the individual that everyone looked when searching for the image of God in man. And it is precisely here that modern theology has taken a new and startling turn; for it now seeks to find the real and essential image of God, not in any one individual at all, but in a relationship between individuals; not in any one solitary being, but only in beings in relation to each other.

Once this has been stated, it appears surprising that no one seems to have thought of it before. For fifteen hundred years now traditional Christianity has been saying that the essence of the nature of the Godhead is a relationship of Three Persons in One Substance. However true the old jest may be which said 'the Father incomprehensible, the Son incomprehensible, the Holy Ghost incomprehensible—and the whole darn thing incomprehensible', there has always been at the root of Christian thinking the fact that God is not solitary. Surely, then, any image of God must be at the very least a relationship of two persons trying to fuse into one.

That is why man is a gregarious animal, why he can never be fully man so long as he is solitary. But there is also a fundamental form of union that goes far beyond mere gregariousness; that is the union which springs directly from the male-female division.

It seems likely that the seed-bed from which this new line of thought has sprung is to be found, as are so many other fruitful ideas, neither in Roman Catholicism nor in conventional Protestantism, but in that Russian Orthodoxy which is having an increasing influence upon the theological thinking world. It is seventy years now since Vladimir Solovyoff lived and wrote, but many of his ideas are, as it were, only now coming home to roost.

Solovyoff starts off with a very strange idea, which again, once it is stated, seems almost painfully obvious. He suggests that throughout the course of evolution something seems to be happening to the universal instinct of reproduction. Fertility, he says, is decreasing and passion is increasing. No one supposes that the love-life of fishes can be anything but a rather cold-blooded affair: yet fishes spawn in their millions. When we come to the higher animals, and to some extent as we go forward to the more highly organised creatures, we find passion making an enormous increase, while fertility drops from a thousand eggs to a litter of perhaps half a dozen or so. But it is when we come to human beings that we find the greatest increase in passion; indeed with us passion steps up into emotion, and even flies away into the realm of the spirit. Yet a 'litter' of only one at a time, or occasionally two, is quite normal; and furthermore this passion, together with all its accompaniments, can be just as strong in every respect when there is no fertility at all; even when there cannot be, and when this fact is perfectly well known to be the case.

He suggests, then, that throughout the course of evolution sex is striving to free itself from mere reproduction as such. The real object of sex, he says, is not just the reproduction of the species, but rather the final emergence of a higher organism. If, as we may suppose, this all leads up to Man, what is that higher organism which human sexuality is striving after? Let Solovyoff speak for himself:

The true human being in the fulness of its ideal personality obviously cannot be merely a man or merely a woman, but must be the higher unity of the two. . . .[1]

This imparts all the greater significance to love as the beginning of the visible reinstatement of the image of God in the material world to . . . embody in oneself and in the other the image of God, forming out of two limited and mortal beings one absolute and immortal personality.[2]

The mysterious image of God in which man was created refers originally not to one separate part of the human being, but to the true unity of its two essential aspects, the male and the female.[3]

This is difficult; it needs thinking out and interpreting perhaps into more modern terms. Yet there can be few happily married couples who could read this without finding in it an echo of something which they truly know has happened to themselves.

Obviously to Solovyoff the key text in the Creation story is not to be found in the first two chapters of Genesis, but rather in that strange and often over-looked text which prefaces the genealogy of the human race in chapter five: 'Male and female created He them; and blessed them, and called their name Adam [Hebrew for Man], in the day when they were created.'[4] God called *their* name *Man* in the day when *they* were created.

But the clearest definition of this idea yet presented has been given by Dr. Sherwin Bailey. In an article originally published in the *Drew Quarterly* in the United

[1] *A Solovyoff Anthology* (S.C.M. Press), p. 164.
[2] Id., p. 165.   [3] Id., p. 171.   [4] Genesis 5: 2.

States, and reprinted in *Moral Welfare* for April 1953, he says:

> As God is a unity of persons in relation . . . Father, Son and Holy Spirit . . . so Man, created in His Image, is likewise a unity of persons in relation . . . male and female . . . thus reflecting in terms of finite existence the eternal being of his Creator. Man in his full humanity is a bi-sexual unity.

Dr. Bailey finds a fuller explanation of all this in one incident in the old story which is usually completely overlooked. It is remarkable, by the way, how, to thinkers who are very far removed from being fundamentalists, the old myths seem to be coming alive in a new way. Dr. Bailey points out how in the first chapter of Genesis we are presented with Adam. The word is of course also the Hebrew for 'Man', but he here appears as what we have always taken him to be, a single, solitary, independent person. There follows then the story of God giving him the woman so that he may no longer be solitary. But something happened to him first; he fell into a trance. The naïve childishness of the story should not blind us to the fact that here we have something of tremendous importance. The 'deep sleep' which God caused to fall on the man was more than just an anaesthetic; for we see that, after the sleep, it is Adam and the woman together who are now named 'Adam', Man. Not until after the sleep was humanity really in existence; in other words, mankind can never remember being, and cannot imagine what it is to be, a single, unrelated, unsexed individual. Mankind is always dual.

One would not expect to find this sort of thing in a

novel, yet in Charles Williams' fantastic *The Place of the Lion* there is a most extraordinary foreshadowing of this. Anthony Durrant in the novel is thinking of the story of Adam naming the beasts. This, we are told, was done by the unsexed incomplete undivided 'man'. All the creatures of the field paraded before him and he gave them their names. This myth is not mere childish fancy; there is deep reality underlying the suggestion of the one intelligent being giving their names to the unintelligent ones. He alone knows the reality of their natures, and thus, by naming them, gives them their reality. The creatures really *are* what Man knows them to be; all the sciences of biology and zoology only add up to this primal fact. Anthony Durrant dreams of this primeval scene, and he imagines the man then trying to find his own name. Adam tried to discover his own reality, and, as he strove, he fell asleep.

> All things were named—all but man himself; then the sleep fell upon the Adam, and in that first sleep he strove to utter his name, and as he strove he was divided and woke to find humanity doubled. The name of mankind was in neither voice but in both; the knowledge of the name and its utterance was in the perpetual interchange of love.[1]

For it is only as thus divided, with of course the possibility of being re-united, that Man has any real knowledge of himself, or, which is even more important, any real existence as the image and mirror of God. But both the division and the possible unity lie

[1] *The Place of the Lion*, p. 162.

in sex. Dr. Gilbert Russell says much the same thing from a different angle: 'Sex is a separation, a "great divide" set in the body of mankind. . . . In that sense marriage is health . . . wholeness and integration . . .' [1]

Dr. Bailey is quick to add of course that both the division of humanity, and also its partial healing and re-unification, run right through all male-female relationships of any and every kind; they cannot be confined to what are usually known as 'sexual' matters. Partial re-unification, and so a partial but very real reflection of the image of God, is thus not only possible, but is intended to show itself in all happy and fruitful relationship and co-operation between men and women. Be it in business, art, pleasure, friendship, etc., every right male-female relationship ('decent' in the proper sense of 'fitting') is a part of this human bi-unity by which alone humanity can be itself.

Of all such possible relationships there is one which, because it can include all the others within itself and yet give something even more intimate, must be regarded as the primal, the archetypal relation. That is the relationship which includes coitus—within its proper sphere as between a monogamous pair. Once this relationship is established, once it functions fully and includes all those other relational aspects which are possible for these two particular persons, then and only then is the most important part of the image of God fully reflected. Only in such a relationship can humanity be seen as fully human. It ought perhaps to be added that such a statement is no reflection on, or denigration of, devoted celibacy, regarded as a special

[1] Gilbert Russell, *The Meaning of Marriage.*

surrender to God offered by, or demanded of, certain persons. We are talking of the natural plane at the moment and looking at humanity as a whole.

Having seen all this, we can now say that the purpose of sex in creation is precisely that separation of humanity into two complementary halves; with the further purpose that, through the re-uniting of the two opposites, there may come a larger and more perfect wholeness, which alone can properly reflect that relationship of Trinity in Unity which is the essential being of the Creator Himself. We have indeed come a very long way from the two traditional answers to the purpose of sex: procreation or individual pleasure. But, indeed, neither of these can ever be separated from sex; they can only be caught up into something larger. Each of them will still remain, but as a subordinate purpose. Omniscience might conceivably have chosen to divide humanity through some other function. In fact the function which was taken over for this high purpose was the existing male-female sexual division which evolution had already imposed upon the higher animals. And when this function was taken over, it naturally brought with it all its existing powers and possibilities, incorporating them now into the higher purpose. Procreation, then, is still the purpose of sex on the biological level. (Indeed, considering that what is procreated is the vehicle of an immortal soul, procreation is itself now raised to a supernatural purpose.) Moreover, individual pleasure is still attached to the sexual function by a natural arrangement of nerves and reflexes. Both, therefore, ought to have their proper place in that common life of husband and wife which is meant not merely to portray, but actually to create, this unity of humanity, this Two-in-One which alone can mirror the Three-in-One which is God.

Accordingly, procreation and individual pleasure both have their purpose, and neither ought to be removed from marriage. Nor on the other hand ought one of these to be sacrificed to the other. But the prime purpose of sex is now seen to be the development of personalities into a union which in some way transcends the individuality of either. Surely it was of some such 'supra-personal union' that Solovyoff was thinking when he talked of the higher organism which sex was ever seeking to produce.

At this point it may not be inappropriate to suggest that this idea could be read into what many would call the most conservative and traditional of ecclesiastical pronouncements, the Papal Encyclical *Casti Connubii*.

This mutual interior formation of husband and wife, this persevering endeavour to bring each other to the state of perfection may in a true sense be called . . . the primary cause and reason of matrimony, so long as marriage is considered not in its stricter sense, as the institution destined for the procreation and education of children, but in the wider sense as a complete and intimate life-partnership and association.[1]

As so often happens in such pronouncements, the last few words seem to take away with one hand what

[1] *Christian Marriage*, Encyclical Letter of Pope Pius XI (Catholic Truth Society), p. 14.

had previously been given with the other. Yet since according to that same authority no marriage can be considered essentially and completely indissoluble without sexual union, it is surely not stretching the interpretation too far to say that (without prejudice to procreation) it is this 'mutual interior formation of husband and wife' which *is* the real purpose of sexual intercourse.

From this point we can now begin to consider the nature and meaning of romantic love, for love, as we have seen, cannot be separated from sex. There were mediaevals who said that love was the lily which sprang from the dunghill of sex. This is not a very flattering description, but we might remember two things. First, that every flower incorporates into itself elements of the dunghill from which it grows. It transforms them certainly; but it needs them in order to be itself. Secondly, that if Mother Kirk has always tended to stress the unpleasant side of the dunghill, that is merely her unconscious prudery. The Creator Himself has made a world in which even dunghills have their proper place: a world in which 'every creature of God is good, and nothing to be refused'.[1]

But we must go further than the mere rejection of prudery. A fuller understanding of sex, such as we now have, may help us to a better understanding of that strange experience which we call 'being in love'. Yet neither sex nor 'being in love' can be seen in its reality until we can see also that which is so often left out of account, the shadow of the Creator of all things looming behind.

[1] 1 Timothy 4: 4.

V

RECOGNITION

FEW indeed must be the men and women who could truthfully say they have never been in love; yet fewer still would be those who could even attempt to explain in any rational way just what it was that then happened to them. The strange thing about romantic love is that, though it is, in our culture at least, an almost universal experience (perhaps only because everyone is conditioned from childhood up to expect it), yet it still retains its ancient incomprehensibility. Repetition never stales it nor can familiarity bring understanding; its infinite variety seems only to confound both individuals and society.

That falling in love may not always be genuine is true enough; for the vulgarisation of the whole concept of love, the misunderstandings and the sentimentalities, are apt to blind and confuse far too many people. Too often they thought they were in love until further and bitter experience showed that they were not; they had only been cheated by imitations. Such a realisation may, alas! often come too late, when the genuine thing bursts upon them in circumstances in which nothing can be done about it. Yet none of these unfortunate happenings can alter the fact that to fall genuinely in love is a possibility for almost every man and woman, and is something that happens at least once in a lifetime to most of them. Indeed, as discussion of the deeper problems involved may show, it may well happen more than once.

But what is it, this thing which bursts upon us and bewilders all our judgements as well as our feelings? Some enquiry into its real and essential nature is necessary if we are going to answer the questions put in the last chapter. Perhaps the first thing to do is to attempt a description of the process and of its more normal accompaniments. There are, as everyone knows, different kinds of falling in love, different degrees of love itself; but of one thing we may be quite certain. Romantic love, as distinct from affection, however strong, always includes what we may call an emotional storm. This fact has a double importance. On the one hand it may help to distinguish love from such things as respect, admiration, affection, etc.; on the other hand it may easily tend to foster the fatal suggestion that the presence of such an emotional storm is by itself a guarantee of the presence of romantic love. That such is by no means the case, many have found to their cost.

For most people the first experience of love is likely to be that which is commonly called 'calf-love': the storm of emotion which overwhelms the adolescent when he first finds the emotional attraction of the opposite sex suddenly concentrated in one real and living individual person. There is a beautiful description of this feeling in one of the Arthurian poems of

Charles Williams, 'The Coming of Galahad'. He
describes Gareth thinking of the time long ago when

> . . . once I seemed to look
> on Logres pouring like ocean after a girl
> who ran in the van . . .
> . . . and she mounted a wind and rode away . . .
> and I found myself weeping there like a fool.[1]

What man is there who at the age of seventeen or
eighteen has not felt exactly like that? Calf-love is
important because, though manifestly not the real
thing (and how the telling of this by adults can hurt
and harm the adolescent!), yet it is a foreshadowing of
genuine experience. Not only do most people find that
when the real thing comes it evokes a memory of a
previous glory, but calf-love can in itself hold great
spiritual possibilities. That is why adults, for all their
cynicism over the whole business of love, ought not to
dismiss it too easily or seem to hold it too cheap.

But there is a possible explanation of both the
strength and the weakness of calf-love that may be of
some importance. R. H. Ward, in his book *A Gallery
of Mirrors*, points out that the person who rouses this
passion is very often a character who is curiously like
the lover. What is even more certain is that the loved
one is quite a different kind of character from the
other (or others) with whom the lover will later on
have genuine love affairs. Is it possible, he asks, that
calf-love is really a mixture of sex-romanticism and
self-love? Is it possible that the person is loved, in the
degree to which the affair rises above mere sex and

[1] *Taliessin through Logres*, p. 71.

F

romantic emotion, precisely because he or she is an image of the self? Maturity and a greater knowledge of the self and its needs will soon alter that; for the mature self, one that has discovered its own essential incompleteness, will desire not a similarity but a complement. In other words, while on several planes the experiences will be similar, and therefore will feel so very much alike, yet the later one will almost certainly gain immeasurably in depth. For it will now be two-dimensional rather than a plane surface. Yet the vision which came with the incompleteness which is inseparable from immaturity may yet be a glimpse, a foreshadowing, of that greater vision which can only be seen later on in life. We are never indeed to deny the reality of any partial vision, nor yet, on the other hand, are we to say that even the greatest of visions is anything more than partial. It is only by keeping a proper balance between these truths that we can hope to come to any real understanding of the nature of love.

The next thing that is likely to be encountered is what has been called 'love's terrible twin-brother'; in other words, infatuation. This is something at which we may have to look a little closer later on; here it is enough to say that it is usually compounded, as to ninety per cent., of merely sexual attraction. To say this is not to condemn it. But it is important to realise that, because genuine love also includes sex, and the emotions of sex are always more or less the same, infatuation can, in the early stages at least, look remarkably like the real thing. But infatuation is a deceiver whom only time and common sense can hope to unmask.

Calf-love and infatuation may in fact be false prophets; but, though they may be false, they are still prophets. This at any rate is what Alaric Jacob calls them in his book *Scenes from a Bourgeois Life*:[1] 'In love there is often a false prophet. The girl who enraptures us calls to mind another who only faintly attracted us before. So when I came to know Miranda Ireton it seemed to me that Mona Foster had been a sort of preliminary burlesque.' 'Burlesque' is unnecessarily cruel; but there remain prophets, and true ones as well as false.

But how does genuine romantic love happen? That there is such a thing as 'love at first sight' few would be prepared to deny. It is certainly rare, probably very rare, but it does undoubtedly occur. While it would probably be true to say that the knowledge that this experience really was romantic love, and not one of its many imitations, does not come until very much later, yet the thing manifestly does happen to some people at least. In one sudden flash of first meeting, often indeed without any actual contact or communication, the knowledge is born that here at last is the real romance. And, as with physical birth, everything else in two lives is but the growth and development of one supreme moment.

Sometimes, on the other hand, and as if to balance love at first sight, love is of very gradual and almost imperceptible growth; while normal experience is perhaps something between these two extremes.

Such more normal and gradual falling into love, in a direction where perhaps we did not expect it, is

[1] p. 174.

delightfully described in the third and final verse of Rupert Brooke's poem *O Love, they said, is King of Kings*:

> And so I never feared to see
>   You wander down the street,
> Or come across the fields to me
>   On ordinary feet;
> For what they'd never told me of,
>   And what I never knew,
> It was that all the time, my love,
>   Love would be merely you.

Another very fine description, the more important because it contains a phrase which is applicable to every kind of genuine falling in love, occurs in Pamela Hansford-Johnson's novel *An Impossible Marriage*. Here she describes, as in the first person, that change of apprehension which made her look upon a very familiar person in an entirely new manner: 'It was upon me suddenly in joy, bewilderment, and something like fear, when, after years of knowing, and of complex but unanalysed friendship, I had looked upon the object of it with new eyes.'

'Looked . . . with new eyes'; that is the core of the experience. This shifting of apprehension, which may come at first sight, or may delay for the thousandth, is the real heart of what we mean by the phrase 'falling in love'. The question which we now have to ask is: what is it which is now seen which was not visible before? What is it that the lover sees which remains apparently quite invisible to everyone else?

Here of course we have to face a difficulty: the only

words which can attempt to describe what everyone
who is in this state is conscious of feeling will be words
which theology will not like. But we may comfort
ourselves by remembering that neither does the world
understand what it means when it attempts to talk
about this kind of thing. The honest truth is that the
scientific-materialist frame of mind (which is the
general mental atmosphere to which most people are
conditioned) is completely at sea when it comes face
to face with the question of love. The world faces
something which possesses a power which, however
strongly it may feel it, it cannot at all explain.

Perhaps psychology can help. C. S. Lewis, in his
exposition of Charles Williams' Arthurian poems
called *Arthurian Torso*, says straight out that romantic
love, like so many other things, has its roots in what
the psychologists call the 'collective unconscious'.
And in this suggestion he only follows out what
Williams himself hints at in what the poems have to
say about the mysterious wood of Broceliande. Broceliande plays a very large part in the metaphysical
conception of the poems, and both writers have a good
deal to say about the whole question of that symbol of
the 'wood' or 'forest' which appears in so many legends.
What does it really signify? In the poems of course it
is pictured as a geographical locality. But what happens there? what comes out of it? above all, what
happens to those who go there? C. S. Lewis answers
that it is in fact the 'collective unconscious', the
'place' or state to which 'Saint, sorcerer, lunatic, and
romantic lover all alike are drawn—Dante and D. H.
Lawrence, Boehme and Hitler, Lady Julian and the

Surrealists, had all been there. It is the home of immense dangers and immense possibilities.'[1] He elaborates this by saying that it is in fact 'what you find when you step out of our ordinary mode of consciousness'. And it is precisely this step into an enlarged and abnormal mode of consciousness which every lover knows he has taken in the moment of vision. The greatest and most matter-of-fact materialist cannot deny that when he fell in love he felt at least as if he had done something exactly like this.

Since this transcendental factor is the core of romantic love, not only in its feeling but also in what we shall offer as an attempted explanation, it might be as well to quote two further remarks upon it. Jean Guitton, in a book which is invaluable for any study of either love or marriage, has this to say about the experience of falling in love: 'The Parisian street-arab who meets a shop-girl, in the most conventional style, with gestures inspired by the local cinema, with words derived from street-songs, may have an experience which, however confused, will remain like a gleam from another world.'[2] Lady Pakenham in her most penetrating essay on 'Marriage and the Family', in the symposium *Catholic Approaches* which she edited, says:

> Just because marriage *is* a sacrament, not a lottery, some inkling of its supernatural nature penetrates to the heart of even the fluffiest little pagan who goes to the local dance hall in search of 'Mr. Right'. Romantic love *à la* women's magazines and 2d. libraries, is after all on the right track. At least it is nearer the truth than the cynical concept of

[1] *Arthurian Torso*, p. 101.   [2] *Essay on Human Love*, p. 194.

the marriage gamble. . . . The teenager at the dance hall
makes no mistake of this kind. A profound certainty grips
her that somewhere, sometime she will meet the man pre-
destined for her from all eternity. . . .[1]

Lady Pakenham calls this a 'partially true vision'. She
is talking of marriage and Jean Guitton of love, yet the
connection between the two is plain, and all the scorn
poured upon cheap literature and the cinema cannot
alter the fact that they may still be on the right track.
The whole point of course will lie in following this
right track: following it to the end and not going off
down side-roads, however speciously attractive they
may happen to be.

A somewhat similar sort of experience would seem
to lie behind the following lines of an unknown Irish
poet:

> Half-kin to the ones that age not,
> The glorious shining Sidh,[2]
> Who flame on the wind-swept mountains
> And dance on the crinkling sea.
>
> But, alas, to the banners passing
> And the glitter of steel we're blind,
> Till their little half-sister, laughing,
> Comes tossing her hair on the wind.

These Sidh are the mythical Celtic nature-spirits, the
inhabitants of Tir n'an Og, the Fairy Land of Youth.
What they may have been originally is lost in the mists
of Irish prehistory. They have now become personi-
fications of the powers that lie behind nature and the

---

[1] *Catholic Approaches*, p. 103.   [2] pronounced 'Shee'.

material world. To anyone at all acquainted with the Irish literature of the 'Celtic Twilight' they will be familiar enough: that is, their mythology can be studied and written about. But no one expects to see them, or even to imagine he has seen them; unless indeed he 'step out of our ordinary mode of consciousness' in that other way which the Irish so pleasantly describe as 'having drink taken'.

But this shifting of apprehension comes entirely through the girl: it is because she is seen in this new way, seen suddenly with new eyes, that they can be seen as well. Not visibly seen perhaps, but known and believed in now entirely because this girl, hitherto so ordinary, is seen for the first time for what she really is, and all along has been: their 'little half-sister'. Because she is she, they are they. Because she is now known, they can be known too. Something appears which was invisible before; and it appears in and through the person—probably first of all through the body—of the beloved.

The modern lover who calls his lady an angel has probably not the faintest conception of what an angel is really like; still less of the fact that, if there are angels, then angels and men are totally different forms of creation. He is using the only word and the only picture he knows in order to describe a kind of being who shows more than its own nature, a power who can open up vistas undreamed of before.

Now in all our complaint about the Church having neglected romantic love, there is one name that so far we ourselves have neglected. That is the name of Dante, who was as certainly a devout son of Mother

Church as he was equally a great lover. But the Church has at times seemed to be highly suspicious of Dante; his sixteenth-century ecclesiastical editors, for instance, bowdlerised him quite shamelessly. (Mother Kirk's fear again?) Yet neither his orthodoxy nor his knowledge of love can really be denied, and we cannot do better than follow Dante's own description of what happened to him when he too fell in love. For that which happened to Dante, described though it be by a poet and a mediaeval, is just what happens to any young man. He may not have either Dante's insight or power of poetic description, but he can and does have Dante's experience.

Dante tells us that, when he first met Beatrice in the streets of Florence, there fell upon him a *stupor*. This Latin word is really quite untranslatable, but it does manage to convey to our minds something of that flash of shifting apprehension, that awe mixed with fear, which the experience of love at first sight always brings.

But to Dante this *stupor* was mixed with reason, with what he calls 'the good of intellect'. We may note that Dante, being a good mediaeval, does the exact opposite to what modern young men in the same situation would do. They, being good materialists, promptly hand the whole thing over to sentiment. Dante, whom they would dub 'benighted, super-stitious and priest-ridden', hands the matter over to reason. He knew of course that reason was not all; but he also knew for certain that real love must have in it the element of reason. Is not this precisely the factor which distinguishes love from infatuation? Infatuation is always in the end unreasonable, while genuine love must include the element of reason. But reason being there in the first flush, one or other of two things can then happen to it. It can be ignored and forgotten, left by the wayside as it were, while the lovers descend the slippery slope into mere sentiment. Or it can be transformed into something else; for transcendence does not exclude reason, it overtops it. If reason be lost, then indeed we are undone; but if no one go beyond reason, then romance itself will die.

The second thing about this *stupor* was that it had an almost physical effect, a phenomenon with which all lovers are familiar. Poets have described it in many ways: 'She walks in golden light', etc. Perhaps the most moving description of all is to be found in Charles Williams' 'The Coming of Galahad',[1] where he talks of someone seeing

> each motion and mode of the princess Blanchefleur
> who walked dropping light, as all our belovèd do.

Poets both good and bad have surpassed themselves in trying to describe what really happens here. And, though no one would say that the 'golden light' is objective, or could be spectroscopically analysed, yet every lover knows perfectly well that this is something that he has seen.

Dante then proceeds to talk about that quality in the beloved which caused the sudden shift of apprehension of which we were speaking: the vision which called her an angel or an inhabitant of the Land of Youth. There comes to every lover, as there came to

[1] *Taliessin through Logres*, p. 73.

Dante, a knowledge of something which is at once she and not she, a vision which sees her as she really is, and yet at the same time somehow larger than herself. Dante named it 'the quality of eternity'.

To go from Dante to the most sentimental of the moderns, it is not long since a crooner was heard—or misheard?—on the wireless to sing: 'This is the kingdom of heaven . . . to hold your hand.' To many listeners this must have seemed perilously near to blasphemy, but one may dare doubt whether Dante, for all his orthodoxy, would have thought so. Certainly he would not have thought so if he had known that these were the only words familiar to our post-Christian generation by which a transcendence of any kind could be described. Had the crooner had any knowledge of what Christians commonly mean by the Kingdom of Heaven, doubtless he himself would have been appalled. Yet we may suggest that he may after all have been nearer the truth in one sense than either he, or his ecclesiastical critics, would have realised.

The last effect mentioned by Dante is not the least important; it is that reformation in manners, and even in character, which the vision of Beatrice caused in him. Beatrice, he says, called forth in him a tremendous humility, a quality for which he had not hitherto been distinguished. Who has not felt the same in the apprehension of the beloved? Not only is the whole world renewed in her, the lover himself is renewed; for the first time perhaps he feels full of goodwill and sympathy towards other people. How do we know that a young man is in love? By his foolishness; yes, but this foolishness often seems to take the form of a great humility (sometimes indeed of a sort of mawkish inferiority), and also of sudden quite unexpected bursts of kindliness and generosity. He feels for the moment at peace with all the world; in all trembling humility he wants to share his joy with all the world. That the world often finds this desire a bore does not deny its reality. Nor does the fact that this change of manners is usually extremely short-lived.

Now there is in all this something that is remarkably akin to religious conversion; the same sudden change of manners, the same emotional accompaniment, and the same kind of reasons given for it. That in conversion the two former results are not always lasting does not deny the reality of either, and the connection between them is indeed highly suggestive. The two things seem to go the same way. Is it because in a sense they are the same thing?

Charles Williams in *He Came Down from Heaven* has a very suggestive phrase which would seem to sum up many of these ideas; he says that in the beloved the lover sees 'the life he was meant to possess instead of his own'. But—and this is the vital point—the lover also knows that this new life is to be a shared one; it is too full to be solitary. She then, the beloved, is the one person who must share it, the one who alone, in the lover's present belief at any rate, can share it. And the shift of apprehension which sees her, and sees this in her, can best be described in the keyword which alone is capable of gathering into one all the various strands which go to make up the experience known as 'falling in love'. That word is 'recognition'.

It is strange to find that it was Solovyoff again

who, if he was not actually the first to use this word, was certainly the first to give it prominence in this connection: 'The basic meaning of love consists in recognising the absolute significance of another person.' Significance for whom? First emotion may suggest 'for ourselves', but even the first flash of apprehension shows a deeper meaning; that of a shared life at least. For if it does not indicate a shared life it indicates nothing at all. Jean Guitton says much the same thing: 'Every cognition will be a recognition. The person loved will seem to be familiar even before being known. . . .' [1] It is true that this is a reference much more to the emotional effect of recognition and its disturbing sense of familiarity, but it points also to a deep truth.

One might make a rather simple parable by imagining a keen small-boat sailor wandering through a boat-yard, and following his thoughts as he looks at the various craft lying there and idly appraises their merits. Suddenly he comes across one that has an irresistible appeal: 'That's the craft for me.' But simultaneously with this realisation there flashes into his mind the vision of the possible voyages to be undertaken in that craft. The whole panorama of sea-life (whether previously known or merely imagined and desired) is suddenly glimpsed and made alive through the recognition of the craft itself. The ship and the voyage fuse in his mind into one vision. This is, it would appear, an almost exactly similar experience . . . which is doubtless why sailors continue to say that they fall in love with certain ships.

[1] *Essay on Human Love*, p. 63.

Now with all this the world will agree, because it is in fact only a description of what seems to happen every time a human being falls in love. It is what every lover at least thinks is happening. Our question now is: what is the reality lying behind? Is there indeed any reality behind, and, if there is, what are we to say about it from a theological point of view?

It is just here that some of the other ideas put forth by Charles Williams may be helpful. There is a sense in which he blazed an entirely fresh trail of thought, and we can well begin by quoting what Heath-Stubbs has to say in his monograph *Charles Williams*. Of falling in love he says:

> Our modern psychological way of thinking, though it must perforce admit that such experiences do happen, would always tend to interpret by means of terms such as 'projection' and 'sublimation'. Williams will have nothing to do with this. Religious emotion is not sublimated, unconscious sex. Rather, every lover is, in some degree, whether consciously or not, a religious mystic.[1]

This must not only mean that theology has an explanation of love, and indeed the only real explanation; it means a great deal more. It says plainly that every lover is, whether he knows it or not, actually putting theology into practice. And this is the core of Williams' teaching on the subject; it is the point of departure for everything that he has to say about either love or marriage, and if we are to follow his ideas out it is here that we too must start. He himself

[1] *Charles Williams* (British Poets series, published by the British Council), p. 21.

would of course have said that he got it all from Dante. The correctness or propriety of his interpretation of Dante is not our concern; that is a matter for the literary critics. What is far more important is that, whether validly derived from Dante or not, here is a set of ideas of which Mother Kirk must now take notice. Here is possibly the one and only key which will unlock the confusions which have come about over the matter of romantic love. Even should these ideas, which seem to us both new and revolutionary, be pronounced largely mistaken, yet the Church can never again talk about love without paying at least some attention to them. Now that they have been put forward, they cannot be side-tracked or forgotten.

What we have to ask is whether theology can explain the nature of that which we have agreed to call by the name of recognition. We suggest that the answer is twofold. First, that theology can give people those basic facts which alone can adequately explain their feelings. Secondly, that recognition is something which religion has always known about, but has not so far admitted into the matter of romantic love.

'Every lover is . . . a religious mystic.' Now what is it that the religious mystic sees and seeks? God, of course, is the simple answer. But it might be truer to say that God was the ultimate object of his quest, and that partial glimpses of God are vouchsafed on the way. 'Seeing God', however, means a great deal more than we commonly suppose; it includes a great deal that mere 'hot-house piety' ignores. It means not only seeing God, but seeing all things in God; that is, *seeing all things as God sees them*. That such a vision would bring with it something that we describe by that unfortunate word 'fear' is all too true; which is precisely what also happens in recognition.[1] Williams himself says that, whereas, with our sentimental ideas of love, we tend to turn God into something like our own sentimental indulgence, 'the meaning of love ought to have something of the "otherness" and terror of God'. But, when genuine, it certainly has this quality, and in so far as it has this, it must be at least akin to the vision of God. 'All things in God . . . all things as God sees them.' But how do we approach this beatific state?

There have always been held to be two ways by which men may come to the Vision of God, two ways in which God may be partly known in this life. Father Neville Figgis in his book *Civilisation at the Cross Roads* called them the 'world-accepting' and the 'world-renouncing' attitudes to life; and he insisted vehemently, not only on the validity of each, but on the necessity of each for a full apprehension of God and His world. Williams, with his insistent concern for what we may call the solidity of the Revelation of God, uses the term 'image' over and over again, and calls the two ways to God, the Way of the Affirmation of Images and the Way of the Rejection of Images. It is fully explained by C. S. Lewis in *Arthurian Torso*:

Holding the first [the Way of Affirmation], we see that every created thing is, in its degree, an image of God, and the ordinate and faithful appreciation of that thing a clue which, truly followed, will lead back to Him. Holding

[1] See Pamela Hansford-Johnson's '. . . in joy, bewilderment and something like fear'.

the second [the Way of Rejection], we see that every
created thing, the highest devotion to moral duty, the
purest conjugal love, the saint and the seraph, is no more
than an image; that every one of them, followed for its
own sake and isolated from its source, becomes an idol
where service is damnation.[1]

Of these two ways of approach to God it is of course
the Way of Rejection which seems the most familiar;
indeed, in Puritan cultures, or in cultures like our own
that are influenced by the overhang of Puritanism, it
is commonly supposed to be the only way. 'Being
good' is thought to be synonymous with 'never enjoy-
ing yourself'. The Way of Affirmation has however
just as great an authority behind it: the way of the
ascent of the soul to God 'through the ladder of
created things'. And Romance, at least in its widest
terms, has also always been recognised as a valid image
which may be affirmed on the way. The Grail
Romances should have taught us that at any rate.
But what is somewhat new, and indeed startling, in
Williams (in spite of the fact that he almost certainly
got it from Dante) is the suggestion that romantic love
can be a proper variant of the Way of Affirmation.

Yet once one has made the reversal involved in
looking at the whole thing upside down, or inside out
(as the world would say), this ought to be obvious
enough. We are to see every created thing as being in
reality an 'image' of God; the thing as God meant it
to be, as showing what He intended it to show: something of Himself. 'There is not', said Father H. J.
Steuart, 'a single created thing which is not, and is not

[1] *Arthurian Torso*, p. 151.

G

meant to be, first and foremost a revelation of Him.'[1]
That is how the Way of Affirmation sees things; how
it tries to use things. And 'things' or 'images' must
include 'persons'.

Now all these strange experiences we have mentioned, the 'life one was meant to possess instead of
one's own', the 'absolute significance of another person',
the thing that was 'she and not she . . . larger than herself', these things which are visioned in the act of falling in love, could perhaps be put more simply by saying that, in the 'shifting of apprehension' *we are now
seeing, in and through another person, that which God meant
Man to be.* We are seeing that person, not as the world
(including up to now ourselves) usually sees them, not
perhaps as they actually are at this moment, but as
they really are in the mind of God. Because we are in
love, that is outside the mode of normal consciousness,
we see something that men and women normally do
not see. And why do we not normally see it? Because
of the consequences of our fallen state; because of
the divided and contingent knowledge which is now
our unhappy lot. It is the experience of most poetic-
minded men and women that we are always haunted
by the half-memory of our former state of innocence
and clear knowledge. Can it be this half-unconscious
haunting which causes the feeling of recognition; that
it is recognition of something that we think we already
knew, something never quite forgotten? If recognition
brings, for the time at least, a simpler state of knowledge, could it not then be described as being able—
allowed, privileged—to see in one person a vision of

[1] *The Inward Vision* (Longmans, 1929), p. 2.

that state in which all men were before the Fall? The state in which they abide in the mind of God? But that would mean seeing them as a means of seeing God; as images. Which is just what the religious mystic does with everything.

This is exactly what Charles Williams says in another passage. He compares Dante's experience of his love for Beatrice with that vision which Milton, in *Paradise Lost*, puts into the mind of Adam on his first seeing and 'recognising' Eve. Eve is to Adam two things, not one; two interrelated things: she 'is at once an inhabitant of the kingdom and the means by which the kingdom is seen'.[1] And what is 'the kingdom' but the Kingdom of Heaven which is *ultimately* the vision of God and of all things in God?

Many would of course say that all this is quite up in the air, that it is only imagination. We might ask the poets to tell us of the precise relationship between imagination and reality; and it would certainly be the reverse of the verdict of the 'practical' world. But anyone can see that, if there be a God at all, in the sense in which any Christian or theistic philosopher would use the word (and we are assuming all along that there is a God), then it is God Who is the source and ground of all reality. Only that which God sees really is. Is not that just what the romantic lover is now doing over one person? Dante would certainly have said that that was what he was beginning at least to do when Beatrice flashed across his path in Florence.

Some have therefore suggested that what we are calling recognition is in fact the great natural means

[1] *He Came Down from Heaven*, p. 66.

of reversing the Fall. At which some theologians will arise in wrath and indignantly deny that there can ever be a 'natural' means of doing this. But we may ask the theologians to remember two things. First, that we are not suggesting that this vision is anything more than momentary. Secondly, that as they themselves always insist, the dividing-line between the natural and the supernatural is extremely hard to define.

The further consequences of such an idea will of course be tremendously important. But already this idea can, if it be allowed, go some distance in explaining those transcendental overtones which always seem to accompany the act of recognition. Lovers, we may say, 'just recognise'. Cannot the Church now step in and tell them what it is that they are recognising, and what the consequences of such a weighty matter are bound to be?

But there is even more than this in the recognition involved in falling in love. Let us return to those theological ideas with which we closed the last chapter. At the front of this book is printed one of the most delightful little love-poems of this century, W. B. Yeats's *The Song of Wandering Aengus*.

> But something rustled on the floor,
> And someone called me by my name;
> It had become a glimmering girl
> With apple-blossom in her hair
> Who called me by my name and ran
> And faded through the brightening air.

Twice is the phrase repeated, 'called me by my name'; and we have seen already something of what this can

mean. Probably Yeats was thinking of the age-old
belief that the real and essential being of anything was
only to be found when its true name was uttered . . .
that belief which for the ancient Jews forbade the
speaking of the real Name of God. He may even have
been recalling, as we did in the last chapter,[1] the story
of Adam naming the creatures. Had he also in mind
Adam's inability to utter his own name because he fell
into that sleep from which he woke for ever divided?
At any rate the connection is plain to us, for what happened to Aengus is just what happens to every lover in
every genuine act of recognition. Who knows my
name? Who can call me by my essential reality?
None on earth at all. Not my friends; not even my
parents . . . certainly not the parents whom most of us
surprise and so often disappoint. None in fact knows
my name but God in Heaven.

But now something has happened; now, in this
flash of recognition, there has appeared on earth someone who *does* know my name. A 'glimmering girl' has
appeared whom I recognise, and who recognises me.
She now does what hitherto only God in Heaven could
do: calls me by my name; sees me as God sees me.
Whether we be charged with blasphemy or not, there
is only one quotation which expresses this mutual
recognition that has now occurred. It is 1 Corinthians 13: 12, and in Mgr. Knox's translation we see
it plainly: 'then I shall recognise God as he has recognised me'. But we suggest that this is not a blasphemy
because the two experiences are not merely alike, they
are in a sense two parts of the same thing. She sees

[1] See p. 62.

for the moment as God sees; she too has made a recognition.

But this indeed means, as Dante clearly understood, that, in seeing her as God sees her, I am permitted a first glimpse at least of that beatitude whose ultimate vision is not merely things in God but God Himself. It implies something else which, if not more important, is certainly more fundamental in change of outlook. The shift of apprehension is not merely a change of view from 'earth' to 'heaven'; it is a shift to a totally different dimension: a different point from which to view either earth or heaven. It is the total and complete change from seeing what I now know to be only half a life (that is my own life as a single-sexed, unrelated individual) to seeing the possibility of a life that is whole precisely because of its essential duality. The new life which is recognised is a life that can only be lived by two-in-one.

Now if Solovyoff and Sherwin Bailey were right in saying that it is only in this duality of male-in-female that the real image of God can be found in Man, then recognition means recognition of this potential image of God, and of its only possible source and origin. She —for we must speak in the singular, and 'he' and 'she' must henceforth be regarded as interchangeable or alternative—is not only that image, through the affirmation of which I am to find the glory of God; she is also that other one with whom alone I can myself be that real image of God that I was created to be. I have recognised the one with whom alone that duality can be found; for I have recognised in her (as she, when she called me by my name, also recognised in me) that other half of what God made to be the divine-human bi-unity.

It is of course not quite so simple as it appears when stated like this; not so simple as love at first sight imagines it to be. There will arise for our consideration, for instance, the terrible question of whether or not there is only one person with whom I can have such a recognition. But whatever answer we find for that question, we can at least say this now; that even the silliest and most sentimental talk about 'meant for each other from all eternity' has grasped this deep truth, that in the bi-unity which is visioned there is a divine purpose, a mirror of the eternal reality of God. The sentimental women's magazine may be astray in its understanding, but it is not astray in its subconscious recognition that such a bi-unity is possible. Nor is it mistaken either in the recognition that this is something which God meant men and women to find: and then—the harder part—to live it out in sweat and effort. That is another and a later part of the story, but this act of mutual recognition is the start of every genuine affair of romantic love.

However, we must now see that our affirmation of the reality of such an experience, and our understanding of its underlying meaning, do not of themselves imply anything at all as to the time or the conditions under which such an act of recognition can occur. The problem of its relationship to marriage will have to be faced; but is it not true that in many cases of rather dull conventional 'arranged marriages' which later on blossom out into love, what has happened is that the recognition has occurred after marriage instead of before it? Why should it not, especially in those cultures which do not expect it before, or which make no allowances for its happening?

On the other hand, of course, recognition does not necessarily lead to marriage. It did not do so between Dante and Beatrice; and it need not have done so even if Beatrice had lived.

Of course there are false recognitions about, and mistaken ones too, and it is these that cause the tragedy and the heart-break. But no number of false recognitions, no number of tragic mistakes, can alter the fact that this recognitional experience is something that seems to be possible for most men and women. It happens to a very large number, and it leads to happiness at least as often as it leads to disaster.

Now is not this matter of recognition a point at which Mother Kirk and the world which has revolted against her could be brought together in some sympathy and understanding? For this is an experience which the world knows only too well. (It is after all for its sake that the world revolted against the strait-jacket, as it calls it, of marriage.) The world knows it; it is half-fascinated by it and half-tortured by it. Fascinated, because it cannot escape from it; tortured, because it does not fully understand it. But if the Church will explain the genuine reality of this experience, it is perhaps possible that the world will listen now as it did not listen in the past. If, on the other hand, she can explain to the world the real nature of what is happening, if she can tell them the facts about what they feel so terribly, she may perhaps be able to keep their feet on the right path.

For there is a path to be followed, a long and sometimes stony one; there is a pattern to be grasped and
understood. It is for all of us as it was for the young
Dante when he was told to 'look well' into the eyes of
Beatrice. He saw the glory and, like a man gazing at
a kaleidoscope, he was blinded by the light. But as
he watched, a pattern began to appear, a complicated
tracery joining God and man, heaven and earth, the
lover and the beloved—and love. The glory is blinding
enough at first sight, but the traceries are there, including all the complexities of life as two-in-one.
Soon, all too soon perhaps, they will begin to project
into life; and then will come the test. We shall find
some of them perhaps as we turn now to look at the
next subject of importance: the dangers which are
inherent in that tremendous shock which we call
recognition.

VI

THE DEVIL'S TRAPS

EVERY recognition has its dangers, for recognition, like every other human encounter, is a challenge. It presents the person at once with a choice of action, and we seem to be so made that it is always easier to make the wrong choice than the right one. This is of course one of the results of the Fall; but the really serious thing about our present state is that, in this as in so many other things, we are quite incapable of seeing that the choice is the wrong one until very much later on. It is not only our will that is weak, our judgement is also impaired; we are not able to see things straight.

Perhaps it was her deep knowledge of these inadequacies of human nature that made the Church suggest, or at least seem to be suggesting, that the Way of Rejection is a safer method of approach to God than the Way of Affirmation. Affirmation of any image involves the possibility, indeed the probability, that a wrong choice will be made. This perhaps may be the reason why it would seem that the Way of Rejection has been over-preached and over-stressed; there are far too many nasty little maps of this way lying about.

Affirmation is bound to involve the possibility of

wrong choice. But the really important thing for us to note is that in this matter of romantic love these dangers do not usually come—at any rate in the first stages—from any outside influence or person. They are somehow inherent in the very act of recognition itself; they are an almost inseparable part of it. If recognition is really in some sort an experience of God, then the Devil will be waiting to trick us back to himself. And he catches us out by some quality that resides in the very experience itself. There are therefore, in all experiences of falling in love, certain things which we can aptly name 'The Devil's Traps'. It is almost impossible not to fall into them, at least partially. That is why no love-affair ever goes altogether smoothly, and why so many, having started in a blaze of glory, go out 'not with a bang but a whimper'. To study the real pattern of love would be to see something of the nature of these traps, and therefore to be warned. If we want to be less theological we could put it more simply by saying that every experience of falling in love is immediately followed by an inclination to imagine love, or to follow love, in a manner and mode which, if persisted in, will inevitably lead to disaster.

The first of these traps is that of being so overwhelmed that we fail to see what romantic love really is. It is a failure to do what Dante said we must do: 'look well'. It is a failure to trace the true pattern of love, perhaps even to recognise that there is a pattern at all. 'The pattern of the glory'; that is the kind of phrase which Dante and Charles Williams and C. S. Lewis would use, and it is as well to see just what they mean. To our muddled way of thinking, glory, and especially perhaps the glory of love ('love in a mist' and all that kind of thing), means something hazy and indefinite. But that is not the original meaning of the term. C. S. Lewis in his book *Miracles* has pointed to something rather remarkable in those strange visions of the glory of the Lord that are recounted in the book of the prophet Ezekiel (chapters 1 and 10). He makes the suggestion that the prophet was possessed of what we would call some kind of psychic power, a kind of supra-temporal consciousness, so that his mind was able to roam about in the dimension of Time. In this dimension, in which he was able to see the future, he looked for some overwhelming earthly thing which could be a picture or mirror of the awefulness of the glory of God and of His Angels. Anyone who reads these visions of his can have little doubt, granting these premises, of what it was that he found. For the image which these visions call up to our mind is like nothing so much as the sound and the fury, the fire and the glitter, of a squadron of jet-bombers roaring overhead. That would seem to be the picture which he found and which was for him a faint reflection of what he meant by 'glory'. But we know well that such a picture is in fact a pattern of mathematical intricacy. The sound and the fury, the fire and the glitter, are in reality steel-hard and accurate to ten-thousandths of an inch.

Must there not be a corresponding hardness and intricacy about the pattern that lies behind the glory of recognition? We are so overwhelmed by the sound and fury, that is by the emotional storm which inevitably—and rightly—accompanies the vision, that we cannot for the moment see the mathematical intricacy of the pattern. But it is there all the same, as indeed it must be in anything which is made by the God Who made all things in hierarchy, order and pattern.

What, we may ask, is the real trouble with human nature over anything? Is it not always the fact that we tend to take the short view instead of the long view; that we rest content with immediate experience and its delights, instead of examining what the experience involves in its real and essential depths?

Everyone would agree that it is just this taking of the short view which is responsible for the wreck of so many love affairs and is the deadly danger of so many marriages in their early stages. The emotional storm of falling in love has been so strong, especially when we add to it the urges of now heightened sexual desire, that it may well sweep off their feet people who are not already sufficiently disciplined. It may very easily sweep them into actions which later on they may bitterly regret. Yet that is only to say that they failed to take the long view. It does not invalidate the vision itself; nor its emotional accompaniments either.

But after all, religion or philosophy is scarcely needed to teach us this. The ordinary day-to-day world finds soon enough that, once people can begin to settle down, once they learn that happiness never comes by direct seeking but is always a by-product of something else, then they are beginning to find traces of a pattern in life. Very soon it will be seen that love can only continue to exist as the generous and self-giving side is strengthened and encouraged, and a path or pattern through the jungle of emotion and desire opens up. And this path must now be followed, or love itself may be lost in the jungle.

Much of this will have to be considered more deeply when we come to some of the domestic problems of married life. At present we are concerned with the vision of recognition and the dangers that inevitably lurk therein. We said in the last chapter that the glory seen in recognition is a part at least of that ultimate glory which is the vision of God. And the first great trap of the Devil consists precisely in the failure to see this; and to know that it is this heavenly thing which has happened. For recognition is a heavenly thing and it is here that Dante can help us again. Dante had not only an angel to tell him to 'look well', he had also what he called the 'good of intellect' or reason. Now Dante's intellect told him that in Beatrice his *salute* had appeared. There has, needless to say, been controversy over this word. The sixteenth-century ecclesiastical editors of Dante were afraid of its implications. They did to him, as we have seen, what Dr. Bowdler did to Shakespeare: altered him in the interests of 'decency'. What he had said seemed far too dangerous. Had he not actually called the lady who went before Beatrice by the name of Giovanna, and said explicitly that she was like the Forerunner, John the Baptist, who went before the Salvation of the world? Beatrice was called *salute*; therefore Primavera must be Giovanna. The editors could not stand this. Yet the purpose of Salvation is to lead to Beatitude, and if there is any sense at all in which recognition is akin to beatitude, then the one recognised is in that sense a real *salute*. There is no getting away from this, and it would be better instead to acknowledge it, and see where it can lead us.

It is here that Charles Williams, as Dante's interpreter, explains the whole thing in one striking sentence. 'The superstitions make heaven and earth in the form of the beloved; the theology declares that the beloved is the first preparatory form of heaven and earth.'[1] (It is perhaps a little bold to suggest that theology says anything at all about a matter upon which so far it has been remarkably silent. But we could say that this is how theology would answer, if it were asked and if it condescended to give an answer.) Surely this sentence presents us with a clue to that first and primal mistake; a mistake which the very nature of the vision itself almost forces upon us. Go back to the crooner's verse quoted in the last chapter: 'This is the kingdom of heaven . . . to hold your hand.' As a literal statement this is not merely untrue, it is blasphemous. It is not the kingdom of heaven to hold the hand of anyone at all. Yet on the other hand it is equally true to say that *to hold the hand of the beloved whom we have recognised may well be the first intimation of, the first tiny experience of, something which will later on blossom out into the fullness of the Beatific Vision.*

'First': . . . 'preparatory': . . . 'form': for the one thing may indeed lead to the other; it may show us as much of the other as we are at the moment capable of seeing. Thus, however far apart both in time and in degree, the two things may yet be connected, and

[1] *He Came Down from Heaven*, p. 70.

may yet be parts of the same pattern. This is what we have to see before we can realise why recognition affects us in the way it does. If the danger of misunderstanding is inherent in the act, then the way to safety is not to deny the reality of the vision, but to 'look well', to examine the pattern instead of letting ourselves be blinded.

Recognition might perhaps be called a pointer; but, if so, the vital question is whether we think that it points only to the beloved (which is what we all tend to think at first), or whether we can recognise that it points beyond the beloved, and through the beloved, to Another. Would not even the strictest theology admit that to experience something transcendent, even though you cannot describe it accurately, even though you describe it completely inaccurately, may yet be a true vision of real beatitude, a window opening on to Heaven?

The danger, the subsequent fault, will be to persist in the inaccuracy. Therein lies the path to Hell, the home of final inaccuracy: for while Hell lies at the end of many roads, it is the beginning of none. That is why, if this particular trap is to be avoided, reason and the 'good of intellect' are as necessary in love-affairs as in any other affairs of life. This examination of the pattern, this unravelling of the real meaning of the vision of glory, is not a small thing: it will take most of a life-time at least. But we can see now in what the first essential temptation consists: it is the desire to rest content with what has actually seemed to happen.

All the above will help to explain the next trap,

which is to assume that it is enough to have known and to have had the vision. It is here of course that there comes in all that disastrous modern jargon about love being 'fate'. This love which is 'bigger than either of us', and whose ravages are thereby supposed to be excused, is regarded by the modern world as absolute. It is assumed to have all the rights; no laws, no moralities, certainly no 'stuffy out-worn convention' must be allowed to stand in its way. That is the modern heresy; founded on the truth of the divine origin of love, but, like all heresies, an exaggeration which may lead to the destruction of the truth.

Whether for unfallen Man the experience of the vision would itself have been enough, we cannot say; we have no knowledge of such a condition. But for us it cannot possibly be so, for all our knowledge is slightly false, all our judgements are impaired. Even things good in themselves are always in tension and conflict, and therefore patterns cannot be followed without severe effort and great self-sacrifice. Things, in a word, will always go wrong because we cannot see accurately enough; there will always be a 'self-desirous spirit which troubles the glory'. It is this spirit, inherent in our present human nature, which makes us fail to recognise the vision for what it really is. But it does more than that. It takes the transcendent glory and, removing it from the pattern wherein it really lies, makes us imagine it as an isolated thing in itself.

Thus we find that, if the vision be left to itself, something will inevitably go wrong. It always does. There are love-affairs in which no further effort is made, or in which the effort is of the wrong kind, and

H

so they drift into tragedy and disaster. When that sort of thing happens, the disillusioned lovers will tend to deny that their vision was ever genuine at all. Or rather they would like to deny it, but they can't. They cannot in their heart of hearts deny the reality that once was; all they can do is to deplore the frustration and waste in which it seems to have ended. Indeed, if half the energy they sometimes spend in this futile repining had been put into 'examining the pattern', that is, into making some effort to grow into mutual understanding, the tragedy might well never have happened at all. Even the greatest of visions, because it is experienced by men and women who are weak and uncertain, must have stability and discipline if its results are to endure. This particular trap of the Devil is only another form of the old, old illusion of those who think that, because holding hands in the moonlight is so great a thing, it is enough for marriage. It is not enough; even a Youth Club Discussion Group countered that when they said that the trouble about the way the cinema presented love was that there was 'too much hand-holding and too little house-work'. It all comes from resting on present experience—which nine times out of ten means present emotion—and refusing the challenge to go on. Yet even more fatal perhaps than the assumption that the vision is enough, is the assumption that it will be everlasting; something that all lovers think and that every love song exemplifies:

Macushla, Macushla, your white arms are saying,
That life is a dream and love is for aye.

No amount of practical proof that it never does last like this, no amount of experience seen in the lives of even the happiest of married couples, can ever convince lovers otherwise. The real trouble is that it is both true and untrue. It will not last 'for aye' in the form in which they have it now. But if we are right, if there is a connection between recognition and beatitude, then there is somewhere a 'quality of eternity' about their love; and this quality, seen first in recognition, must in some form or other, just because it is of eternity, endure at least for the whole of life.

It all depends upon how we define a 'quality of eternity'. Here only the most exact theology and metaphysics can help us. Despite the fact that theology and metaphysics seem to the ordinary man to be all up in the air, it is only their distinction between 'eternal' and 'everlasting in time' that will unravel this particular tangle. That which is 'eternal' *always is*. It always is, even though, like the sun hidden on a cloudy day, or even permanently cut off by a concrete roof, it is not at the moment, and indeed may never be, visible or tangible. On the other hand, 'everlasting in time' really only means 'lasting a very long time'; and a thing which lasts a very long time indeed (even for the duration of the whole physical universe) need not of its own nature be 'eternal'.

It is true that Man, the 'child of Time', can only picture or imagine eternity as something that lasts for ever in time, but that is a difficulty of the imagination, and the distinction must be kept clear in our minds, for it is of very great importance in this business of love and recognition. Feelings do not last, cannot last, in spite of all the Macushlas, and reason will inevitably say so; that is, if reason be asked. Yet the lovers are surely right when they say that there is in their love something which is eternal of its own nature. What is this eternal thing? Not, it would seem, the apprehension of the vision, for they will soon discover that the way by which eternal things are seen on earth is not a pattern of 'seeing for ever' but rather one of appearance and disappearance. Dante showed us not only this pattern in an extreme form, but also the real quality of eternity which lies behind the shifting strands of appearance and withdrawal. Beatrice was seen and the recognition flashed between them. But in fact Beatrice was only seen for a short time in their extreme youth; and then her presence was removed by death. The visible Beatrice disappeared, only to reappear in the vision of Paradise many years later. Beatrice, considered, that is, as apprehensible, did disappear, but something of her remained. This was her authority; her authority over him, the authority of their love and of what that first vision had made visible. All this remained as the prime and guiding motive of life and thought; and it brought him at length out of the dark wood and back to Paradise.

What is eternal, then, is not the seeing of the vision or the presence of the vision, but that reality which is measured by its authority over us. The first demand, the first trace of the steel-hardness of the pattern of love's glory, which the vision of recognition lays upon any lover, is the demand for submission; a submission which is made not to the emotions of the moment, but to the authority that lies behind them. This is the first and terrible demand: a demand to stand aside from immediacy, a step which the short view never wants to take. How can it? The very thrill of vision holds us back. Hence the trap, inherent in the very nature of the experience itself.

But the word 'authority' will bring to mind another word: fidelity. This is commonly set before us as a moral virtue, and it is true enough that its practice will involve moral struggle. But one may suggest that, in the context of romantic love, fidelity is not so much an extraneous virtue tacked on to a totally different experience as an essential part of the experience itself. Dr. Sherwin Bailey has written that 'love, of its own nature, demands fidelity'; even on the plane of purely human experience he is right. After all, if there has been a genuine mutual recognition (if each has known the 'name' of the other), then there must be something that inevitably ties the two together as neither could ever be tied to anyone else in the world. Recognition sees this; and the experience of recognition, the feeling and will and emotion that go with it, mean and desire precisely that. There is, and must be for ever, some intimate part of the one that belongs exclusively and permanently to the other. This is so, and every lover determines, quite instinctively, to keep it so.

What precise part of the personality (if personality can be divided up at all except functionally) is the determining and exclusive factor, will depend on circumstances. It may be the purely 'spiritual' or 'imaginative' part; but if recognition follows its normal path and leads to marriage, it is obviously the sexual part of the personality which is delivered exclusively to the other. And fidelity means the keeping of this part, whichever it be, exclusively for the other; or rather it means the *intention* of doing so. Human nature is weak, and intentions often fail. There are many wives who realise that, while their husbands may have committed adultery through weakness or under stress of intolerable temptation, they have never really departed from an intention of fidelity. It is even apparently possible, amongst persons who sincerely reject conventional ethical or religious concepts, for real fidelity of spirit and intention to persist, even though the properly exclusive part of the personality is being promiscuously shared and wasted. Such instances confound the theorist and appal the moralist; but human nature knows well that they exist. Nevertheless they still, in their own half-hearted and twisted way, witness to the fact that recognition always demands a fidelity of some kind. Fidelity is the translation into temporal life of the quality of eternity inherent in recognition. If the intention of fidelity be not there, then we may well question the genuineness of the recognition.

No one will deny that it is extremely difficult to transform the romantic feeling that 'love will last for ever' into an intention of submission to an authority that will remain whatever may happen to the feelings. Of course it is; and chiefly because of the emotional storm that accompanies the act of recognition, which is an inescapable part of it. It is, as we saw a moment ago, this difficulty inherent in the experience of recognition that makes the trap: a trap which the

Devil, we might say, set there in order to tempt us to kill our love rather than to train and nurture it.

We referred to the thrill of recognition; and we are so made that sexual desire is a very important part of that thrill. There is nothing wrong in this at all, but it does provide the basis for the next trap. This is a temptation that does not come until a little time after recognition, but which nevertheless arises out of what were its effects at the time: for the temptation is to prolong the experience, to force some kind of repetition. The accent of course is on the words 'force' and 'some kind' of repetition. We have seen the vision, we have, to use the other simile, affirmed the 'image'; but, as with every other thing met with on the Affirmative Way to God, the image, while given *to* us, is not *for* us. But the thrill of shifting apprehension, the thrills of our sensitive nature that follow naturally upon this (and properly and rightly too), these thrills make us desire to use the image to our own satisfaction. The desire to re-experience the thrill is not wrong in itself; but 're-experience' so soon comes to mean 're-experience for our own satisfaction', and that means 'use'. Very soon it will mean a desire to use only one part of the image. And so almost insensibly there will come a steady downward progression. First the effort to prolong, to force the prolongation of, the moment: then to prolong the lesser parts of the moment; and then the gradually growing appetite for the use of these lesser parts in themselves. Finally we find ourselves, and often to our complete surprise, seeking sexual satisfaction in complete isolation, having shed, almost imperceptibly, the 'good of intellect'. (It is worth noting that our modern separation of coitus from conception is an obviously powerful factor in this downward progression of separation.)

But the real tragedy, indeed the real sin from the moral point of view, lies not, as the Puritans so often thought, in the satisfaction, but in the separation. And it is precisely separation that we have accomplished. There is a lengthy description of such a downward progress to be found in Dante's description of the lovers Paolo and Francesca in Hell. We should note that these two are not in the Infernofor sensual indulgence as such, but because of a wrong yielding to such indulgence, a refusal of what 'adult love demanded'. Their love was illicit, but it should be obvious that this refusal is one that could equally well be made by any canonically united couple. For it is the sin of separation; mutual indulgence soon becomes separate single indulgence; repetition of what the solitary individual enjoyed is increasingly demanded, so that in the end the unity which was foreshadowed by recognition is denied and split back into twain. The 'image' has ceased to have any real connection with That Which it imaged.

There seems in all Charles Williams' poetry to be only one real description of sexual irregularity, and this one is all the more striking. It occurs in one of the Arthurian poems about Lancelot and Guinevere, and speaks of

> the raging eyes, the rearing bodies, the red
> carnivorous violation of intellectual love.[1]

[1] *Taliessin through Logres*, p. 59.

It is easy to misunderstand this, for it is almost certainly not intended to be a description, in the good old-fashioned way, of the difference between 'carnal' and 'spiritual' love. By 'intellectual love' he does not mean what is commonly, but of course quite wrongly, called platonic love: an affection of the mind or spirit with no sexual accompaniment. What he means is true romantic love as Dante understood it; but romantic love that has 'looked well' and has followed the pattern. Love that, by the 'good of intellect', has seen and submitted to the eternal authority lying behind the vision; love joined with fidelity. And this is just what the Arthurian lovers are breaking. Nor is the indulgence called 'carnivorous' because it is sexual, or connected with the desires and emotions of the body. It is not because it is of the flesh, but because it devours the flesh, that their love is condemned. The fleshly desires and emotions are, in their proper place, a part of the pattern of the glory. But here they are precisely out of place; for instead of being a means of union with fidelity, they are being used solely for a gluttonous self-satisfaction. Again it is not satisfaction that is wrong, but *self*-satisfaction separated from any other ends. But how easy to try to force the repetition of the first thrill of recognition, to forget, or never to make time to learn that, as Anne Ridler tells us in *The Golden Bird*:

By faith, not by feeling, is ecstasy commemorated.[1]

This leads on to the final and ultimate trap, that of assuming that the vision glimpsed in recognition is a

[1] 'Travellers' Tales' in *The Golden Bird and Other Poems* (1951), p. 30.

personal possession: personal either to the one experiencing it or to the other. The latter illusion leads
of course directly to the crime of jealousy; while the
former is that incontinent gluttony for the person who
is the vehicle of the vision, which leads in the end to
separation. And really, in spite of all that the old
ecclesiastics may have said, sex in itself may often be
the least of these temptations. The satisfaction may be
highly spiritual: but jealousy still remains gluttony.

For this is a forgetting of what the image is for. If the
image (and this really applies to anything at all, as
well as to the person of the lover) is something to be
affirmed and used as an approach to God, then it
does not, in the usual sense, exist *for* anyone. It is not
ours, although, by God's largesse, it be given to us.
Dante put the matter in his sonorous Latin, and in a
way that is extremely difficult for the modern mind,
untrained in scholastic terms, to follow, when he
wrote: 'Unde est, quod non operatio propria propter
essentiam, sed haec propter illam habet ut sit'—'Hence
it is that the proper operation does not exist for the
sake of the essence, but the essence has its being for the
sake of the operation.' Rudyard Kipling put the same
thing in a much simpler form when he sang that 'The
game is more than the player of the game, and the ship
is more than the crew'. We might explain it all by
saying that God did not first create Dante and then
look round for something for him to do. God created
the possibility of great poetry, of romantic love and
the poetry of the Way of Affirmation, and then
created Dante so that he might, if he fulfilled his
vocation, write of them. The images exist in their

own divine right, and it is when we realise that they are images that we realise also that in a sense we ourselves only exist in order that we may serve them. It is this theme which lies at the back of the interpretation of the Arthurian saga which Charles Williams gives in *Taliessin through Logres*. The thing which is wrong with Logres, the root of all the dreadful evils which are to follow, is a wrong thought in the mind of Arthur the king. There is a moment when Merlin foresees all the doom to come because he sees what is wrong with Arthur. He sees Arthur debating in mind the question: 'the king made for the kingdom, or the kingdom made for the king?'[1] and he sees Arthur's mind answering it the wrong way—and so the total loss of Logres.

For Arthur was wrong; kings exist for kingdoms, sailors exist for ships, cricketers exist for cricket, poets exist for poetry—and lovers exist for love. The vision, the image, the glory—call it what you will—does not belong to either person, *but both persons henceforth belong to it*. That is the clue, and that is precisely where so many go wrong.

It may be worth noting how, in this connection, the experiences of falling in love and of religious conversion are so extraordinarily alike, even to the traps which the Devil sets in the way of each. Those who undergo the experience of conversion find all the glory and the wonder which we have associated with recognition. In its original meaning they have found the truth of 'I shall know even as I am known'. They experience the sweetness and the uplift, and a feeling of love for God, often extremely emotional. All sorts of

[1] *Taliessin through Logres*, p. 21.

things happen to them; peace descends, strength comes against temptation, their prayers are wonderfully 'answered'. The pattern looks exactly the same. It is the same, even to the final trap of the Devil. For people are converted for God; we exist as Christians for the sake of God. But how often does the convert either fail to see this or forget it? The pattern of the convert whose religion is seen by those outside to be all compounded of selfishness and self-satisfaction, who goes to Church only so long as he 'feels good' or the particular service 'satisfies' him, is all too familiar. But the fault is the same; it is the idea that 'the kingdom was made for the king'. They imagine that their conversion was for their own advantage or glory. But it never is; it is always for the glory of God. In just the same way romantic love is not given primarily for our own satisfaction; it is given for the service of love.

Doubtless other similarities could also be found, for we are suggesting that love, whether of God or of man, or of God through the 'image' found in a recognised human person, is always of the same essential nature. The pattern is the same all through because the two loves are not after all sundered.

Perhaps Mother Kirk knew this all along—perhaps? She has taught, in Catholicism at least, all the traps that will beset the feet of the religious convert. (It is the weakness of much popular Protestantism that, while it has insisted wellnigh *ad nauseam* on the necessity of conversion, it has almost completely neglected to call attention to the traps.) Maybe she knows also of the traps which will equally inevitably beset the feet of the romantic lover. She may have turned aside because she saw the dangers too clearly. But the result has been fatal. For by turning aside she has allowed the world to fall under the domination of the most sentimental version of romantic love without any idea of its dangers. The world has discovered the vision of love, but it has largely failed to see the pattern —except at the cost of terrible experience, and often much too late. The Church ought to know the pattern, for she ought to know beatitude in all its forms. Can she not begin to tell the world? And can she begin by saying that all love is from God? That is why it has a pattern; why it has authority: and that is why the pattern must be followed.

VII

THE GRAND EXPERIMENT

Love is the desire and pursuit of the Whole.

PLATO

BECAUSE recognition is an encounter between persons there must always be some purpose behind its challenge. Because it may also be a thing of divine origin, its purpose also may be what we call divine. Different couples of course may have to work these interrelated purposes out in different ways, but the general pattern would seem to be divine as well as human, heavenly as well as earthly.

Recognition itself, we said, is not enough, and imagining that it is so is one of those disastrous mistakes into which the very thrill of love tends to make us fall. But if it be not enough in itself, what is it that ought to follow? Possibly Jean Guitton can give us the answer:

In the last century Michelet understood how fallacious it was to study love in its opening phase alone and not to write its whole life-history. 'If love is no more than a crisis', he said, 'the Loire might equally well be termed a flood.' ... it is true that marriage is the fruit of love; it is still more true that love is the fruit of marriage. And the art of loving is not in the least merely a gathering of the fruits of voluptuousness as Ovid, Catullus and the libertine tradition supposed; it is rather the science of making the fleeting love of youth endure and multiply through the course of a long human life.[1]

Here we have another condemnation of that trap of the Devil which we defined as the attempt to force the prolongation of the crisis by the mere repetition of its more sensitive part. But that earlier phrase 'its whole life-history' gives us the suggestion that the crisis itself is not unlike that other fundamental crisis of birth. And indeed it is; for both are climactic, both are shattering, and each ought also to be only a beginning. Unless the possibilities be allowed to unfold, unless the pattern be revealed more and more clearly, then, as with a new-born living creature, the life will wither and die.

This symbol of birth is a very suggestive one. How many lovers have said that, in the crisis of falling in love, they feel that they have been 'born again', have entered into a whole new world, a fuller dimension of existence! Love poetry is full of such similes, and the poets after all only write of what everyone feels. And here again we note that curious parallel to the religious experience of 'conversion', whose very terms indeed are used. All along we find how these two things, religious experience and romantic love, run side by side and help to complement and illuminate each other. The truth is that neither can be really understood without the other. And yet Mother Kirk has tried so desperately hard to keep them apart.

But birth of course implies growth, development and

[1] *Essay on Human Love*, pp. 88 f.

training, all that Guitton means by what he calls the science of fostering the new life born at the moment of crisis. There is a word here which Charles Williams uses more than once and which seems to be what we are looking for. He talks of 'a great experiment' following upon love.[1] Elsewhere he calls it the 'grand experiment'.

It is a word full of suggestion, for recognition, having a purpose, must be a call to do something, to make some great venture, to undertake some great experiment. But an experiment is always something whose actual results we cannot as yet foresee; it has to be undertaken in faith. And yet we are compelled to make it, we cannot escape from it. But the thing which compels us is just the authority of what we have already seen. Such words apply equally to the explorer passing the 'point of no return', to the scientist hovering on the dangerous fringes of nuclear fission, to the religious mystic flying naked into the 'desert'—and to the lover. It is just such an unseen and unknown experiment which love demands, to which recognition calls us, once the Devil's traps have been overcome.

'We belong to each other,' say the lovers, for that is what they feel at the moment of recognition. At once, as we have seen, there comes the terrible choice symbolised in the lines: 'the king made for the kingdom or the kingdom made for the king?' This is the crucial choice, because upon the way in which it is answered all else will depend. We have seen the wrong answer, so fatally easy. But once the right choice has been made (and we should note that in either case it is

[1] *The Figure of Beatrice*, p. 15.

scarcely ever a matter of deliberate thinking; it is done at some much deeper level), then the lovers realise that they belong, not after all to each other, but to love. And this, we realise, means that, however ignorant or formally irreligious they may happen to be, they find they belong to God. 'We belong to each other' is what they said at the beginning. 'Yes, you do belong to each other' is the answer we must give, 'but only because you both belong to God. And it is because you belong to God that He, out of His largesse, has allowed each of you to see each other for an instant as He sees each of you.' That must be our answer, and it is one which they will accept because, however irreligious they may be, it touches a chord of their own experience.

But an answer like that has further implications. It means that they have somehow dimly seen, not only each other as God sees them, but, incarnate in one person, a vision of the way in which God also sees all men. It is the half-consciousness of this that can explain both the power and the terror of love: things of which the world is only too aware, though it can find no explanation for them.

'Lovers belong to love'; and therefore they have to turn themselves into that thing to which they belong. That is the experiment, the grand experiment that is laid upon them because they both belong now to an authority which will not be content with anything less than the surrender of the whole personality. 'The imagination,' says Williams, paraphrasing Dante, 'determined to actualise within itself the thing seen outside.' That means that, from being *in* love they have to become *loving*: in a sense, become love itself. Once the purely selfish or self-gratifying motive is rejected, there is nothing now left but complete and utter submission to that love which claims them both. They must from henceforth go on 'experimenting' wherever that love shall lead them. What we have now to try and find is the pattern of that leading.

Solovyoff said that recognition was recognition of the absolute significance of another person. Once the indulgence of our own feelings or comforts has been by-passed, then the time is bound to come, even to the most irreligious, when the beloved will be loved and valued, not just for herself alone, but for the things which she signifies. The things which are seen and known in her, incarnate in her character, reactions and behaviour, will soon appear as the only things of lasting worth and value. In religious language that means they are seen as eternal; and she therefore is seen as God sees her, appreciated as God appreciates her. That which was only temporary in the first abnormal, half-unconscious flash of recognition, is now beginning to become habitual. The 'image' is now doing that which, for those who follow the Way of Affirmation, it was all along intended to do. It is becoming for them a pathway to God.

Now all this can lead, and indeed ought to lead, to a gradually growing appreciation of the worth, value and absolute significance of others. The lover must start by realising that his own image is of no more importance than that of the beloved (indeed we saw that his own image was totally incomplete without hers). This then ought to lead on to the realisation on his part that his image is of no more importance than any-one else's. The first thing that the following of the pattern of love will teach anyone is that love can never be solitary; it only exists at all because it is shared between two people. But now the vision can widen and deepen. The really great lovers who have risen above self-gratification in however spiritual a form, are always people of increasing sympathy. For what is seen and fully known in the beloved begins to be seen, dimly perhaps at first, in other people too. First: 'we belong to each other'; then 'we belong to love'; and so on to 'others belong to love'. And so the lover comes at last to the point where he can see that all others belong to love: that is, to God.

The more the practice of the grand experiment leads to the abnegation of self—which it must do, as we shall see in the next consideration—the more possible will this expanding of the original vision become. Loving means living for another; or rather it means both lovers living for something else. In the end, then, it can only mean both living by and for The Other, however in fact they may imagine or name Him.

Dare we suggest that it is this final vision and practice which is the whole divine purpose of the original birth crisis of recognition? For this is just what happened to Dante. Dante came at last to Paradise, and there in Paradise he saw men and women in all the beauty and reality of the glory by which each of them is an 'image' of God. But the thing which brought them there, which bound them together there, was love; as it was also only love which gave Dante himself the eyes to see them. But, in spite of all the theology and 'churchy' language, we must never forget that the first place in which Dante himself had seen love was in the eyes of Beatrice. It was plain and simple romantic love, as we understand and feel it, which was the start of the whole matter. He looked once into the eyes of Beatrice, the eyes of the little girl in Florence (Yeats's 'glimmering girl' who called him by his name), and then in the end he saw those same eyes mirrored somewhere else: in the eyes of the Gryphon, who is the symbol of the Twy-Natured Incarnate Whose Name is Love for all the world. To Dante therefore the road [from the recognition of his *salute* in the streets of Florence to the full Salvation and Beatitude of Paradise, though lengthy enough, was absolutely direct. Following the pattern of love led from loving one to 'loving' all, from seeing 'heaven' in one person to seeing all persons in Heaven.

But Beatrice died. And all this can happen to any man even though his Beatrice 'die'; whether by this we mean physical removal from the earth or only separation from him: death or the impossibility of normal consummation. The vision once having been seen and its authority accepted, that authority being eternal, the pattern can still be followed. And there are many lonely bachelors and spinsters whose loving and sympathetic lives are shining examples of this. It does not always happen of course, and it is the soured ones whom we see more frequently—or at least notice more frequently. But the former exist all right, mute reminders of the fact that the grand experiment can have spiritual fruit even though it be denied the physical. And it began as it always does, with romantic love.

All this implies something which we can only call by the name of 'faith'. Submission of any kind, any worth-while experiment, must involve faith. It is as Anne Ridler has already told us: the turning away from gluttonous indulgence (whether of sensual feelings or of more spiritual repining) leads at once to that other road wherein 'By faith not by feeling is ecstasy commemorated'.

But if we wish to find how this faith works out in practice when Beatrice 'lives', we shall find it best expressed by another word, a word which we strongly repudiated earlier on. There is a strange line in Charles Williams' other sequence of Arthurian poems, *The Region of the Summer Stars*, where he talks of a condition 'when love was fate to minds adult in love'.[1]

It is true that this line occurs in a description of the 'Company of Taliessin', a sort of inner ring of Christians who are working out the real meaning of *caritas*, people who by one pattern or another—that is, by Affirmation or Rejection—have come to that state which we have seen may be the end of the grand experiment. Yet while this line does not refer exclusively or specifically to romantic love, it is hard to imagine that it would exclude it. Indeed it surely must include it in what mathematicians would call a 'special case'.

In an earlier chapter we said that the most dangerous of all modern heresies was that *idée fixe* that every crisis of love (and this usually means

[1] *The Region of the Summer Stars*, p. 34.

only an emotional crisis) was a sort of 'fate' about which nothing could be done. But the line from the poem surely means something rather different. After both recognition and the right and self-surrendering choice based on recognition have been made, then, and only then, love and its pattern and the making of the experiment together have, for both the lovers, become their only destiny. And just because such an experiment cannot of its own nature be anything less than life-long (nor indeed end successfully anywhere short of at least the lowest Heaven), so, for the two undertaking it, it has become what we can only call their fate. Their very faith, the fidelity to which they are now committed, makes the experiment now their 'faith-fate'.

We ought to note in passing, by the way, that 'adult in love' has of course nothing to do with intelligence or scholarship, any more than had that 'intellectual love' which was violated by separation in the Devil's trap. 'Adult in love' means being just what Paolo and Francesca were not: under the way of the 'good of intellect', able and willing both to examine the pattern and to follow it. It is a matter of responsibility and discipline rather than of intelligence, and indeed may often go hand in hand with a good deal of childlikeness on the part of one or both.

But if Beatrice 'lives', then the grand experiment means a life in partnership. We did not specifically state on page 116 that when Williams used the term 'the great experiment' he was referring to marriage and to the conditions which the Church seemed to have thought wise to make over that particular form of the experiment. But this is in fact what he was referring to, and normally it is to the experiment of marriage that the crisis of recognition ultimately leads. And if we examine the pattern of a happy and successful marriage we shall be able to see both the kind of thing which is involved and also the kind of thing which results. We shall see what the grand experiment of a life-time together, based on an original recognition, can lead to. And if it is poetic insight and interpretation that we want, then it is again Anne Ridler who can help us best.

She talks first of that Devil's trap so hardly escaped by any of us, the effort to prolong what seemed happiness by a repetition of its most sensitive but least enduring part, and of the real thing which love can bring out of the avoidance of this. Real certainly, but not always understood or known:

> (For in love we grasp more than we thought to reach
> By God's grace), but because they subject it
> To the wrong tests, and lose while they dissect it.
> Expecting, too, to be perpetually aware
> Of happiness, when the full consciousness is rare:
> For it is our common and strange condition
> Not to know what we are, nor when we are in heaven.[1]

Happiness is a by-product, and this is one of the first lessons of practical married life. But what is that thing of which happiness is a by-product? What is that condition of being in heaven of which we are not aware at the time but which we only discover afterwards?

She tells us that the thing which eventually comes

[1] 'Epithalamion', in *The Nine Bright Shiners*, pp. 37 f.

out of a real union of living together is not either of the things for which we naturally looked at the moment of recognition. And yet, like the happiness by-product, it is something which was really implicit in all that recognition meant:

> . . . but if we look either
> For complete union with the being of another,
> Or for the separate fulfilment of the self,
> We see neither.[1]

It is obviously not the separate fulfilment of the self, which is what mere sensuality or spiritual pride may wish for, but which is the denial of love. But on the other hand neither does the love of man (any more than the love of God) lead to complete annihilation. Those unions in which the personality of the one is completely overwhelmed by the other are not the happiest. It is not the 'henpecked husband' who is held up for our admiration.

No; the surprising thing which really happens is the emergence of a new factor compounded of both. It has even been called a 'mystic third person'. Sober prose may find it hard to define, but every one of us has been touched by its reality every time we crossed the threshold of a happy home, even a childless home.

But let Anne Ridler go on:

> . . . the texture of love
> Is of both, indivisible; something is made
> By lovers which neither singly could.
> A complex result, and as hard to define
> (Though with singular ecstasy known)

[1] Id., p. 38.

And to the eye as little apparent
As the effect of an electrical current.
The inert metal is active, changed
By a borrowed force, and the two are merged;
Yet the life is its own, with which it is charged.[1]

How many modern sermons, one wonders, have been preached in which this symbol of the inert wire and the current which makes it live has been used? But almost certainly it was used as a picture of the life of the Christian in Christ: either the new life of the individual Christian soul, or the life of the corporate Body the Church, both of which spring from the power of the risen Christ Who dwells in them. Only one phrase can describe what Christian teachers, from the time of St. Paul on, have felt about this: 'interpenetrating personalities'. But this poem is not about that at all, and yet it shows exactly the same thing, 'interpenetrating personalities'. And this describes the recognition of romantic love working itself out in the daily practice of the grand experiment. Love and religious experience again go the same way and each illuminates and explains the other. For just as the real Christian is a new creature because of the interpenetration of his life by the life of his Lord, so in marriage each of the partners is merged: but merged not so much in each other as in that 'new person' who arises out of their union.

Charles Williams would of course have used his favourite word 'co-inherence'; and again the parallel would have been complete. For it was his constant

[1] Id., p. 38.

theme that the Church was the 'company of the co-inherence' because she herself was derived from the co-inherence of the Divine Trinity and of the Two Natures in the Incarnate. And here in marriage is Anne Ridler saying that the grand experiment is just the putting of co-inherence into daily life. But as this is done, the new and greater third person will emerge.

But of this co-inherence there would seem to be not one but two possible results, according to whether the interpenetration is merely physical and, as it were, accidental, or spiritual, which must of course include the physical. For all couples living together do in fact form a co-inherence of some kind. Our watered-down remembrance of Christianity has not only removed the terror and the 'otherness' from religion; it has made us think that what is spiritual must be good. We have totally forgotten the possibility of spiritual evil, and so opened the door wide to its entry. It is not therefore only in the good unions, the happy and successful marriages, that we can see co-inherence in practice. What about those unions of which we say that the marriage has fatally broken down; that there is 'nothing left'? Unfortunately there is something left; and we have only to see the two persons together to discover what it is. Each of them is so often charming, kind and sympathetic with other people. But put them together and they bring out at once the very worst in each other. They succeed in creating an atmosphere that is worse than either of them separately, worse even than the sum of their individual selves. Co-inherence is still there, but it is now co-inherence gone sour. If the co-inherence of a happy couple can make the atmosphere of the home angelic, we have to remember that merely physical union and co-inherence can produce something remarkably like a devil. For to refuse real spiritual co-inherence while persisting in the conditions which demand it, is to follow the direct road to Hell.

But the acceptance of spiritual co-inherence, the seeking for it or the allowing of it to grow, can only come, as every married couple learns soon enough, by a great deal of what the world calls 'give and take'. 'Give and receive' would be better, for true love never just *takes*; it gives, and in giving it receives into itself. But it is this mutual giving and receiving which is the beginning of a process by which the one learns increasingly to live by the very life of the other. Separation begins to die. Each one has to submit his or her own will, first in small things and then in greater—or is the process not very often the other way round?—to the will of the other. That is what it seems; but really it is submission to their joint will, the new will of the 'mystic third person' which emerges in due time. But this fulfilment comes only when each has in fact substituted his or her own will, not to the mere personal will or whim of the other, but to the will of this emerging new entity. (It is when this process glaringly fails that we get such aberrations as the 'henpecked husband' or the 'too submissive wee wifie'.)

The key word is 'substitution'; a substitution by which I live only in and through her, and she lives only in and through me. (How close again is the parallel to religion and 'I live, yet not I, but Christ liveth in

me'!)[1] That is what happens when all goes well; and
it has a rather strange result. There is a great deal in
Arthurian Torso about freedom: a freedom which seems
to be the negation of this kind of substitution. But
the theme of the writers is precisely that 'willed
servitude *is* freedom'. We have here an echo of those
puzzling ideas of St. Augustine on the same subject.
St. Augustine startled many by suggesting that, while
not to sin was a freedom, the greatest freedom of all was
not to be able to sin. Not to sin was, of course, to
exercise one's choice ('freedom'); but to be unable to
sin was the perfect response of a perfectly free personality to the holiness of God. The authors of *Arthurian
Torso* are applying this idea to a perfect human relationship. Plato said that love is the desire and pursuit
of the whole. Lovers are meant to seek for and to
make a new kind of Whole which is perfect freedom
and which can only arise out of the perfectly willed
surrender and substitution of the two of them. Each
must merge completely into the other, not for loss but
for fulfilment. Out of the willed servitude of the two
separate persons can arise the perfect freedom of the
new emerging whole, the perfection of response to the
perfection of love. But it can only come as mutual
substitution is complete, and such mutual substitution
always begins with the humdrum process of 'rubbing
along together'.

There is no need to preach theology about this, for
it is the everyday experience of millions of married
couples. But theology may perhaps help to explain its
real meaning by shedding some light on the total pat-

[1] Galatians 2: 20.

tern of love. And it could well illuminate this process by showing its extraordinary likeness to other processes which are normally considered as only for the specially pious. But God, we forget, has no favourites.

From now on there will be need to refer to some of the much earlier poems of Charles Williams, which are comparatively little known, many indeed of which have long been out of print. Literary critics do not speak so highly of these earlier volumes, but for the purpose of following out Williams' particular ideas on romantic love they are of the very first importance.

Take, for instance, this whole business of substitution. In the very earliest volume he ever issued there is a little poem in which he describes the house of Love where there is said to be

> . . . a little door,
> Narrow, low-arched, and carven thereabove:
> 'Through me by losing shall a man find love.' [1]

'He that loseth his life shall find it' would seem to be as true in the matter of romantic love as in religion. But it could only be so if romantic love were indeed one of the 'images' on the Way of Affirmation.

Perhaps the greatest significance can be found by setting together two poems, one from each end of his literary career, and with presumably the whole of his married life lying in between. In one of the poems in *The Silver Stair*, published in 1912, there is the following description of what we are calling the crisis of recognition:

> When suddenly thy coming shook the air,
> Thy presence rose upon me as a light

[1] *The Silver Stair*, p. 50.

> Whereby I knew my way and came aright
> Unto the house God chose me of His care.[1]

In 1938 was published *Taliessin through Logres*, the first book of Arthurian poems, and in this we find the following description of what he calls co-inherence or substitution:

> that the everlasting house the soul discovers
> is always another's; we must lose our own ends;
> we must always live in the habitation of our lovers,
> my friend's shelter for me, mine for him.[2]

It is of course the word 'house' that supplies the link over the twenty-six years. 'House' presumably means 'state of being'; and the state of being to which falling in love led, the end of the road upon which love had suddenly shed its light, is the state of being wherein we can only live by substitution.

But the joining of the word 'friend' to that of 'lover' is surely an explicit reference to the idea, implicitly hinted at in the phrase the 'Company of Taliessin', that romantic love is only a special case of something far wider. The grand experiment begins, it is true, with the special case; but from what has been learnt in the practice of substitution in daily life (the actual working out of the experiment) the co-inherence of all men in Christ can begin to be understood. For the end of the experiment is to change half-glimpsed theory into known and experienced fact.

Now all this, which is after all nothing but ordinary experience illuminated by the theology of the pattern

---

[1] Id., p. 32.   [2] *Taliessin through Logres*, pp. 44 f.

of love, suggests two things. First of all we might ask whether we may not now have discovered that of which Vladimir Solovyoff was thinking when he talked about the 'higher organism' which the reproductive instinct was always striving to reproduce. Sex, he said, was striving to free itself from mere reproduction of the species as such and, all through the scale of Evolution, was concentrating on the higher organism of the next stage. But what, we asked, could this be in Man? especially as sex remained equally strong when there was no physical result at all. Is this the 'higher organism' he was after, this new co-inherent personality which derives from substitution? Here is a new free personality emerging out of the willed servitude of each of the two lovers; is not this the higher organism which Man, separated into male and female, is capable of producing when male and female are joined?

Furthermore, if this be so, we now have that real image of God of which Dr. Sherwin Bailey talked. Recognition found the person with whom this real image of God might be made (and may possibly, in that state of being 'out of the ordinary mode of consciousness', actually have seen something of that image), but it is the long labour over the years of the grand experiment which has made the image actual in the world. Nevertheless it is there, and so we must insist over again that if this is what any couple make out of their life together, then they are glorifying God whether they realise it or not. They are, as we have already said, acting like religious mystics, strange and even repellent to them though the term may be.

Perhaps the clue to the whole matter is to be found in that rare place where extremes meet and what seem opposites are reconciled. One of the most difficult of the poems in *Taliessin through Logres* is called 'The Fish of Broceliande', and it deals with the matter of Bors and Elayne and their sudden falling in love at first sight. Bors falls in love with Elayne and the symbol of his love (how like Yeats and *The Wandering Aengus!*) is a fish that he seems to see flickering up her arm. It is not a real fish in the normal sense of the word. In another sense it is even more real, for it is a fish of 'Broceliande', that wood we may remember which symbolises the collective subconscious, 'the state of being outside the mode of normal consciousness'. It is the state into which lovers, and others, pass; and in that state Bors sees the fish: the hidden meaning of the vision of recognition. But this fish, like other fish, has a forked tail, and, as he looks, he sees these two forks flicker in opposite directions:

> . . . one, where the forked dominant tail
> flicks, beats, reddens the smooth plane

> of the happy flesh; one, where the Catacomb's stone
> holds its diagram over the happy dead
> who flashed in living will through the liquid wish.[1]

To see the really startling suggestion here we must remember that the diagram over the Catacombs was also that of a fish; 'ichthys' which is the acrostic of Christ crucified. It stands over the graves of the

[1] *Taliessin through Logres,* p. 25.

martyrs. The martyrs are those who have made an entire substitution; those in whom 'my Eros is crucified'; those who say, as all lovers say, 'Another for me and I for Him'.[1] But the two forks, the happy flesh (of married coitus?) and red martyrdom, are parts of the same tail. It could seem to lead to both ends alternatively, or even simultaneously. Is not the pattern of love always that of substitution, though every person works it out in a different way?

If we were now to take together the various results which seem to flow from the grand experiment we should find that there was only one term which could describe them at all adequately. The widening vision that sees all men as God sees them; the complete co-inherence of one person in another by which substitution is both practised and learnt; the servitude that blossoms into a fuller freedom; the complete substitution of the self into a larger whole, whether of marriage or of martyrdom; all these are the marks of what the Scriptures call *agape* or *caritas*, the New Testament revelation of love. The manner of life of the grand experiment then is substitution; but its matter is that enlarged vision of living by another; and these two things together are *caritas*.

Have we then at last found the connecting link between the two things which Mother Kirk has for so long kept apart, romantic love and *caritas*? *It looks as though the aim and end of the grand experiment is precisely the transformation of romantic love into* caritas? Is not the grand experiment one way of doing that which some are called to do by the Way of Rejection, others by

[1] C. Williams, *The Descent of the Dove*, p. 46.

K

martyrdom, and others again by the Affirmation of images of a different kind?

That such a thing is a possibility seems very likely; and if it can happen at all, then no number of failures can alter the fact that we may have found the connecting link. The possibility is now wide open to all those who will take the hard road of following the pattern to the end.

In an earlier chapter we suggested, with some hesitations, that the shifting of apprehension which is the vision of recognition was the great natural means of overcoming, or going back on, at least one of the effects of the Fall. To this we may now add that the making of the grand experiment, following upon a recognition, is the great natural means of learning about and achieving *caritas*.

And this time without any hesitation; for not only is the line between the natural and the supernatural always hard to draw, but Catholic theology has always said that every man who truly desires the grace of God can receive it. The ignorant and the 'irreligious', so long as they follow what light they have and with real effort trace what pattern they can recognise, will always be granted God's 'uncovenanted mercies'. Indeed, who is to say in any given situation how much is natural and how much is the grace of God, whether covenanted or uncovenanted? That the pattern of love which follows on a genuine recognition can lead to a state that is quite indistinguishable from at least the beginning of supernatural *caritas* seems undeniable. So we may well ask whether in fact this is not the real aim and purpose of the whole business of sexual division, sex attraction, romance, romantic love and the grand experiment. One thing leads to another in an orderly progression, so that we ask if this be not the pattern that was 'in the beginning'. If so, then the Church and the world are closer together than we thought at first. And someone ought to tell them so.

It is here also that we can begin to see where the indissolubility of marriage enters into the pattern. Love of its own nature, we saw, demands fidelity; and the grand experiment demands a 'faith-fate'. But human nature is weak and our judgement is impaired; so we are at the mercy of our feelings, of circumstances, and indeed of the sometimes bewildering changes of the pattern itself. There is need therefore of an institution which can safeguard this fidelity, and bring sanctions, when necessary, to enforce this 'faith-fate'. Such an institution, such a skeleton or binding structure, is provided by holy matrimony and its permanence. Hence we may say that marriage is the normal way of making the grand experiment; permanent marriage is meant to be the grand experiment in being.

But this of course is true only in part, for it must be repeated that it is not at all necessary that the Way of Affirmation, nor even one kind of grand experiment, should involve marriage: remember always Dante and Beatrice. It is true that to attempt the experiment without marriage brings many difficulties; but marriage brings difficulties of its own. Still less ought we to let anyone imagine that every marriage is automatically a matter of the grand experiment. But normally speaking, marriage that follows upon falling in love provides for the majority of mankind the means whereby they can most safely and profitably work out the pattern of love in the grand experiment. Perhaps this is what love and marriage are for.

VIII

WITHDRAWAL

WE have now shown that genuine love always follows a pattern. We have also tried to show something of the nature and purpose of this pattern and how it works itself out through the ordinary experiences of falling in love and getting married. These things the world does, but all too often moved by an obscure instinct rather than by any knowledge of what either involves. On the other hand, we have tried to show that they are in fact the expression in actual day-to-day life of that pattern which exists 'in the mind of God'. We have pointed also to the similarity between falling in love and religious experience, a similarity so close that one might say that the two things were but two sides of the same pattern. Perhaps they are not even to be as much distinguished as are the two sides of a coin.

Human beings fall in love; that is, they make a recognition. They become engaged; and get married. Such is the normal course, and, after that, married life can gradually transform their love into that higher, but not separate, thing which Christians have learned to know by the name of *caritas*. It all sounds so simple when put like that. And, in spite of the official blind eye which for centuries the Church seems to have turned upon romantic love, we may yet believe that countless thousands of Christian, and indeed of semi-Christian and pagan, lovers and happily married couples have in fact lived the experiment out in this manner. Whether or not they could see clearly what they were doing, they have put the pattern into practice, and have thus actualised into daily life that bi-unity which is the image of God in Man. And, thank God, they continue to do so.

But, except perhaps for the most fortunate, it is not quite as simple as all that, for the pattern of love is more complicated than would appear at first sight. Going back to that idea of the mathematical hardness and rigidity of what we mean by 'glory', we may say that this pattern has many more sharp edges than we bargained for. To follow it out, to 'look well', will be to come up against them; the pattern can never be experienced in all its fullness without a sharp experience of their cutting edges. 'And so they lived happily ever after' may be a good ending to a fairy-tale, but as the ending of a romance it is simply not true. Unless indeed 'happily' be interpreted in a much wider and deeper sense than usual.

And so, having explored the real meaning of falling in love and the real purpose of the grand experiment which is meant to follow upon the vision of recognition (being indeed the very purpose of the recognition), we must now go on to consider two problems which are almost certain to arise in any normal married life. These two phenomena are so common that they might well be considered as being parts of the pattern itself.

We shall again find a great deal of help from the ideas of Charles Williams, for he was perhaps the first thinker to face them both squarely and to attempt an answer from a definitely Christian point of view. If these ideas are in any way correct, then we may also find that we have hit upon the real explanation of two things which, when they occur, so puzzle the world. They not only puzzle it, but, unless guarded against, they are capable of breaking up or destroying many a marriage. If by doing this we can help people to see what kind of pattern is to be expected after marriage, if we can explain the real meaning of some of the factors which may be expected to trouble any marriage, then we shall have done something very much worth while.

We talked a while ago about the 'death' of Beatrice; by which was meant the removal of the accessibility of the person of the beloved, whether by actual physical death or by circumstances which make normal consummation in marriage impossible. And we saw that this did not, and indeed need not, mean any death or withdrawal of what we called the authority of the vision. But there is another type of withdrawal possible; that is the withdrawal of the vision, or 'image', while the person continues to remain visible: sometimes in fact all too visible. It was, we may remember, one of the traps of the Devil to make us think that the vision itself would be 'everlasting'. It will not be; it never is. What is eternal is its authority, and this eternal authority is quite compatible with both the appearance and the disappearance of its visibility. We said, in so many words, that the pattern of the vision

of love seems always to be 'one of appearance and disappearance'.[1]

The vision then will be withdrawn, but not by the
death or removal of the person. The person remains;
it is the vision which will fade out and seem to die.
There is a very striking verse in one of the volumes of
Charles Williams' early poems, which talks of a similar
sort of withdrawal of religious feeling which is often
experienced by the devout. The poem in question is
entitled aptly enough 'On Leaving Church', and it
describes that all too common experience of coming
home from Holy Communion and immediately falling
into a rage because the breakfast is not cooked to our
liking. (This too we are apt to call a trap of the Devil,
but it may be that it is really a permanent part of a
pattern we have failed to recognise.)

> The sacred ministers are gone,
> The royal banners furled;
> And we, our dullness putting on,
> Are left unto the world.

Dullness; that is the great enemy of ecstasy, whether of
religious feeling or of romantic love. And unless we
can remember that 'by faith, not by feeling, is ecstasy
commemorated', we shall fall straight into the trap in
either case. Dullness; so different from all the words
which we wanted to apply to the vision of recognition
or to the grand experiment which followed it. So
different also from that word which, even though we
were not used to religious terms, we wanted to apply to

[1] See above, p. 104.

the crisis-vision of recognition: the word 'glory'. 'Glorious' is what falling in love was, and surely 'glorious' is what the grand experiment itself also ought to be. Glorious is probably what it was during the first few years. But glory has hard edges, and dull, dull, boring and full of ennui is what it has suddenly become.

R. C. Hutchinson in his interesting novel *Interim* makes one of the characters, a Roman Catholic priest, use this very word when discussing with another character some of the problems of marriage. The priest had called marriage glorious, and had been hotly challenged for using such a word about something that led to so much disenchantment. But his answer is: 'A man sweating in a quarry is glorious, but there's no enchantment about him.'

Another Roman Catholic priest has spoken very wisely on the same matter. Father Gerald Vann, O.P., has in more than one of his writings shown us that the Church, even in her most conservative circles, has more knowledge than we suspected about the pattern of love and marriage. He too is talking of what we may call the 'quarry-sweating stage' of marriage when he writes as follows:

It is not easy out of all these things to make a union which is real and deep and personal. It must at best be a long process; and it must include darkness. After the *vidi* and the *amavi* there will have to be the *credidi* before the perfect love is achieved . . . love is a mystery, and human sex is a mystery, and the body is a mystery; and so they all have to be learnt slowly, gradually, lovingly, patiently, humbly, like a poem or a symphony; and it is *thee* I worship with my body, the real person, this human being with these faults and weaknesses.[1]

'Slowly, lovingly, patiently, humbly': only so can the pattern ever be followed. But Father Vann has put his finger on the real root of the trouble. For it is the essential humanity of the beloved, now seen ever more clearly, which, because it is necessarily an imperfect humanity, itself so often causes the disappointment. It is seen, and it has to be lived with. One would hesitate to say 'has to be endured', but in the extremest cases this is just what has to be done. And this is the cause of that malaise which turns glory into dullness. 'Love is blind', so the cynics say; but it is not true. All that we have said so far suggests indeed that in the vision of recognition, far from being blind, we are for the first time seeing the essential reality of a person. But this vision of what is 'eternal' has now to be balanced by the knowledge of the essential humanity of the person, that temporal humanity which is the day-to-day clothing of the vision. God may have designed it as a robe, but too often we see it as more like a shroud.

In one of the rather rare humorous passages in his prose Charles Williams makes the young man Anthony Durrant say to his lover Damaris: 'You are the Night of Repose and the Day of Illumination. You are, incidentally, a night with a good deal of rain, and a day with a nasty cold wind. But that may be merely Allah's little game.' [2] It is not often that men and women see both the eternal and the tem-

---

[1] Gerald Vann, O.P., *The Water and the Fire*, p. 123.
[2] *The Place of the Lion*, p. 30.

poral aspects of any person so clearly at first recognition. But after several years of living with the nasty cold wind anyone may be forgiven for thinking that they have reached the 'quarry-sweating stage' of marriage.

The normal marriage may probably be expected to pass through several such stages, and to recover from them; for that never-forgotten authority lying behind the vision may bring the partners through. Indeed, that faith by which alone ecstasy is commemorated will probably bring most people to another stage wherein—on the appearance-and-withdrawal pattern —there may be a further, if different, manifestation of the glory. But sometimes it is a desperate matter which, to those experiencing it, seems utterly final.

Once the authority of the original vision is suffered to diminish, and this is only natural to weak men and women, then it is on the appearance alone that we shall tend to concentrate; on the visibility, the person alone. But it is precisely the new and more intimate knowledge of the person that seems to diminish the glory. The greater knowledge leads to disillusionment, and disillusionment breeds boredom and ennui at the very least. What is needed then is to go on clinging to the authority in spite of the new knowledge, indeed to try and make the new knowledge a vehicle for that same authority. But no one is going to pretend that this will be anything but a painful process.

There was once a tactless lecturer who told an audience of spinster women that single life was a martyrdom. Amid the laughter that followed he only saved himself by adding that, as a married man, he

knew by experience that married life was also a
martyrdom. He explained that, for a Christian, any
state of life must be a martyrdom in the proper sense
of the word, 'witnessing at cost'. We have already
quoted[1] that strange passage in which Williams suggests that martyrdom and its complete substitution are
a parallel to the course of love and its grand experiment (whether fulfilled in marriage or not), but there
is a much better word we could use, if only its meaning
were not so easily misunderstood. That is the word
'purgatory' or 'purgation'. The idea of married life as
a purgatory, while acceptable enough to the cynics
(especially perhaps the married ones), is a suggestion
that will be hotly denied by most married people. But
that is only because they have a totally wrong conception of purgatory, one that is bred into them by
the emotional overtones of past religious controversy.
What do we really mean by the word 'purgatory'? A
cleansing and purifying of the character by which it is
made fit to behold and share in the glory of Beatitude.
If that is so, then the real object of purgatory is, as
both Dante and Charles Williams hinted, 'to make the
singular plural'. It is the taking of the single, separate,
independent and almost completely self-centred soul,
and uniting it with God. It is the process by which
Divine Love makes out of one solitary being a new
being compounded of the surrendered soul and the
Divine Love of God in Christ. This is a completely
religious concept. But even those who say they do not
understand it, or who think that it has nothing to do
with them, can and do realise something else out of

----

[1] See above, p. 133.

their own difficult experience. They discover soon enough that to make a union of two-in-one, to turn two independent singulars into the plural of a happy marriage, requires a deep and continuous purging of each individual's sharp corners. Here again we find a parallel between the grand experiment of romantic love and the process that follows on religious conversion. They are exactly similar, and neither can be anything but painful. Both proceed in the same way, by loss as well as by gain, by hard roads as well as by smooth, by what seems dullness and boredom as well as by ecstasy.

We think that it is the image which is being purged or which we are losing. What is really being purged is our own mind which sees the image. It is being purged so that, in the end, it may see the image, whether of God or of the loved one, the more clearly.

'Loss' is what we feel. But we have to remember that loss and limitation are themselves 'images'; that is, experiences of the created world by which, as by others, we may hope to come to the full knowledge of the Creator. But to be 'affirmed' they must be experienced; that is, they must be felt as what they are; and they are loss and limitation.

C. S. Lewis, commenting on some rather strange lines in *Taliessin*, asks whether it is not a fact of experience that, in the service of all masters, it is just when help seems most needed that the master seems to give no help at all. 'The fullest grace can be received by those only who continue to obey during the dryness in which all grace seems to be withheld.'[1] He

[1] *Arthurian Torso*, p. 154.

adds, what may be familiar enough to students of theology, that 'God gives His gifts where He finds the vessel empty enough to receive them'.[1] But it is also true of earthly masters, and of 'mistresses' too, in the proper sense of that much-abused word.

There is surely something here of immense importance; something which seems to have been largely missed, alike by lovers tortured by doubt and disillusion, and also by those pastors and theologians who cannot see beyond the confines of what they narrowly define as the 'spiritual life' (meaning too often by that term that which flies away from the world of real experience).

If this were a devotional treatise on the well-documented Way of Rejection (what is known as the Negative Way), all the above could pass as a perfect description of what the mystics have called 'The Dark Night of the Senses'. Is it possible that the pattern of love is always the same, for the Way of Affirmation as for the Way of Rejection; the same for Divine Love as for human love? May it not be that in the service of romantic love, no less than in the service of God Himself, no one can come to that state of willed servitude which is freedom without passing through such a purgation, without coming to, and passing out of, a stage of dryness in which there is nothing at all to make us go on except a blind faith in the authority once submitted to? God of course is such an authority; but so also is the vision of recognition in a human being. Is not then the withdrawal of the vision into dullness, boredom and disillusion, which occurs to

[1] Id., p. 156.

some extent in every marriage, an exact parallel of the Dark Night? Is it not exactly the same phenomenon under a different mode?

But no one ever talks to people like this, to those who are in love or to the newly married. Just as in the same way no one ever seems to tell adolescent Confirmation candidates that the time will come (probably after a year or eighteen months) when they will see nothing at all in their religion. The time will come to all of them when they will begin to say that they see no point in it any longer: 'it does them no good'; 'they don't feel any better for it'. They will see no reason why they should go on attending dull and dreary services. And so they will cease attending, and we shall be well on the way to the usual seventy-five per cent lapse which most parishes have learnt to expect from the newly-confirmed. And all because no one ever told them that this time of dullness was the real test of faith; the first step towards that *willed*, as distinct from merely *enjoyable*, service which alone is the real freedom.

And so it is to some extent in every marriage; the time of testing and disillusion will come. It may be short or long, merely irritating or nearly disastrous, but come it must for that is how the pattern goes. But no one ever tells the newly-wed what to expect; no one ever tells them that this is the inevitable purgation that turns singular into plural (or two into one, for we are dealing here with a transcendent phenomenon that can only properly be described in contradictories), the only way of coming to the willed service that is freedom, the 'quarry-sweating stage' of glory and beatitude. So it is that marriages begin to waver and slide towards

the rocks; and when a new emotional crisis with someone else makes its appearance (and of course it always
chooses a time like this to appear), then it looks as if the
grand experiment had failed. As a result they think, in
true modern fashion, that a fresh experiment is thereby
indicated.

Such an experience certainly seems to suggest
failure; the whole thing seems to have dwindled away
to nothing—or worse than nothing. The seriousness
and length of time of these periods of withdrawal will
of course vary enormously in different cases. In
religious experience Dom Chapman warned us that
such a state might well last for twenty years or more;
and there seem to be some marriages about which
almost the same thing could be said. In such cases the
couple, under the sway of the false emotionalism and
romanticism of our age, are almost bound to say that
they have failed. But have they failed? Can they—can
anyone at all—really tell? Human happiness rarely
comes by direct seeking; it is usually a by-product of
something else. C. S. Lewis, again in *Arthurian Torso*,
says that while every 'Logres' fails, yet some minor
by-product of the original design usually survives. Now
no one is going to suggest that every experiment, even
when founded upon the most genuine of recognitions,
is inevitably going to produce the perfect result. To
very many it may appear that 'some minor by-
product' is now all that they can hope for. But who
except God can ever judge what is major and what is
minor? This is exactly the state of mind of Edward
and Lavinia in the second act of T. S. Eliot's *The
Cocktail Party*. Edward, seeing, as he thinks, his mar-

riage almost in ruins, says that he supposes that all
they can do now is to 'make the best of a bad job'. He
is answered by Reilly who tells him the exact truth:

> When you find, Mr. Chamberlayne,
> The best of a bad job is all any of us make of it . . .
> Except, of course, the saints . . .
> You will forget this phrase,
> And in forgetting it will alter the condition.[1]

That is, what seems to be only the best of a bad job
according to the original, and only half-understood,
vision (for the glory blinded us) may be that true and
original pattern which we are now so painfully
finding.

There is in fact only one set of couples which can be
quite certain that it has failed. This is the one which
has fallen into the Devil's trap, which made the
immediate reversal of the vision, and has stuck to
that. Those who have said that the kingdom was for
the king, and have taken love for their own selfish
delight. Of the rest, of even the most feeble, we must
say that they know not how they build; at least until
the time comes when the true pattern of every human
life be seen in full.

For a really full understanding of that part of the
pattern which we have called 'withdrawal', for a guide
through some of its troubles and complexities, we must
turn again to those earlier poems of Charles Williams.
There is, first, the continuation of that poem already
quoted, 'On Leaving Church', when 'we, our dullness
putting on, are left unto the world'. We saw this as

---

[1] *The Cocktail Party*, pp. 111 f.

L

applying equally to the withdrawal of the vision after
several years of married life. But, we may ask, what
happened in the poem after the return home? and the
answer is rather surprising.

> Yet at our table, even then
>   Of common food what grace
> Adorns that outer world of men
>   In your possessèd face;
> Where, watching with the Holy Ghost
>   I see our Lord fulfil
> His outer dwelling, yea, almost
>   He is there visible.

Here then is the recalling of the first vision of love as
seen in the face of the beloved, of what had been
glimpsed in that first sudden shift of apprehension: a
recalling that is now made entirely by faith. Faith,
under the dullness that has inevitably been put on,
still sees the 'glimmering girl'. The original vision,
however, was of something more: it was a sudden
glimpse of unfallen Man. But unfallen Man was himself a 'first preparatory form' of the Incarnate: and it is
the vision of this which faith now recalls and describes,
in language which to some would doubtless seem
blasphemous. But any charge of blasphemy must be
equally levelled at Dante when he tells us that he saw
the eyes of Beatrice reflected in those of the Gryphon,
symbol of the Incarnate. To see all this through the
inevitable dullness of the years may indeed not be
blasphemy but eternal truth.

We turn now to a series of poems from *Poems of
Conformity* with the title of 'The Christian Year'. The

idea of this must have come from John Keble, but it is an interpretation of the Christian year which would have shattered Keble, for it is an interpretation in terms of romantic love. (Yet did not Keble himself in his happy marriage experience it all?) There is a quite deliberate likening of the progress of the grand experiment in marriage to the incidents of the Life and Passion of our Lord. Naturally enough what we have called 'withdrawal' is made to correspond to the death of the Lord. To us, who know the full story, Calvary is but the prelude to the Resurrection. We have, however, to remember that it was not at all like that to those who actually experienced the loss on the first Good Friday evening. It is of them, and of them in that despairing state, that the poet is thinking. And we must note very specially who the person is, and how he is described, who is called upon to bring strength and power to the disciples during the post-crucifixion period of withdrawal:

> Bring us, O John his lover, home at last:
> Time yet must be, and we fulfil our past.
> Us to thy guardianship he hath decreed
> True friend, Morality . . .

To fulfil the past, to wait in darkness, to know the vision gone and wait for its reappearance (if indeed one does wait, for while the promise had been made to the disciples they, like disillusioned lovers, were quite unable to understand it); all this will need something like the grimness of pledges and vows. It may well need even the service of morality and convention just to force us to stay where we are to avoid scandal. Any or all of these can be, and are meant to be, of inestimable value in holding together couples in whom, against their own knowing, the grand experiment is actually being worked out.

There is another poem in which the matter is put far more clearly. This poem is so important, and also so comparatively unknown, that it must be quoted in full. It comes in the volume *Poems of Conformity* and is called 'Ascension'.

> The tides of Christendom begin,
>   The years of faith and hope,
> A cloud of days receives him in
>   As our Lord Love goes up,
> Still from disseminating hands
> Bestowing blessing on our lands.
>
> We shall not find him here again,
>   Who felt his first surprise;
> No loneliness or thrill of pain
>   Shall draw him from his skies;
> Nor shall a second Wonder smite
> Our eyelids with so much of light.
>
> A cloud of days receives him in,
>   God unto God returns;
> To his profoundest origin
>   Love manifested yearns.
> But now he was! but now, my Fair,
> Flickered his presence in your hair.
>
> O look, look! ere that presence dies
>   The Spirit's flame is here,

Descending in new mysteries
　　Ere Christ can disappear,—
In whom all living must be shared
That great Nativity declared.

All things he shall in order due
　　Bring to remembrance; he
Infallibly shall hold us true
　　And indefectibly.
Incredible is this to prove?
Ah, how incredible was Love!

A cloud of days receives him in,
　　That Christ of yesterday:
The years of faith and hope begin,
　　While we must watch and pray.
Our Church her mission hath received,—
We know in whom we have believed.

Council and law shall hold us fast
　　And ritual shall grow stale,
Yet sense of this assurèd past
　　Shall mightily prevail,
For in your face the Holy Ghost
Kept—how long since!—his Pentecost;

When, darkly burning in your cheek,
　　The rushing blood rode high,
Yet felt its soul and it too weak
　　To bear the same God nigh,
Who, on the Apostles being come,
Enlarged them into Christendom.

There are of course two separate strands here, but they
are so closely intertwined that it is sometimes very

difficult to tell which is being spoken of, and indeed sometimes both together are meant. We may believe that this is wholly intentional, a parable of the matters themselves. The first strand is an attempted explanation of the experience of the Apostles (and, through them, of the historic Christian Church, which is organically one with them) by which they, having lost sight of their Lord at the Ascension, were, in the power of the Holy Spirit at Pentecost and after, transformed into what we call Christendom. They are shown in fact as having received their Lord back again, but through a new, enlarged and different experience. This is of course traditional Christian doctrine; what is so startling is its application to everyday life in a totally unexpected manner. For the second intertwined strand is a description of the progress of a happy and fruitful marriage. It is a picture of that pattern whereby two lovers, bound to each other by the original vision of recognition, are, by a different experience, by loss as well as by gain, by faith, by hope and remembrance, themselves transformed into a totally new kind of wholeness: a wholeness which he elsewhere calls by the apt name of a 'twy-nature'. (But we should note that Twy-Nature, with capital letters, is how the Gryphon, the Incarnate in Whom are fused the Natures of God and Man, is also described. Here again is the same parallel.) [1]

The interesting thing, however, is the difference between this and the poem previously quoted. In that, the withdrawal was pictured by the death of the Lord, which was the prelude to the Resurrection and the

[1] See p. 120.

appearance in far greater glory. But here it is pictured by the Ascension, after which there was no visible appearance at all. There are indeed couples who seem to be called to marriages rather like this, though the normal experience is not so trying.

'And a cloud received him out of their sight', and that repeated refrain, 'a cloud of days receives him in', hammers into our brain that repetitive dullness which must inevitably obscure every kind of romantic vision which has to be lived out in the trivialities of daily life. Whether the vision be of love or of God, it must vanish into the cloud of days. But what happens then?

The real heart and clue of this poem is the conception of 'Christendom': the transmutation of the single separate Apostles into the coherent body of the Catholic Church. In order to understand this, and to see its application later, we must accept at least the idea of the *Corpus Mysticum*, that is the Church as the living body of Christ. Now before Pentecost the Apostles were separate individuals, each with a *personal* love of the Lord. Each one of them separately was in much the same state as is the romantic lover at the moment of recognition; each had as it were 'fallen in love' with the Lord. But now by the operation of the Holy Spirit (Who, being a Person of the co-inherent Trinity, is Himself the Lord) they are merged and enlarged into the co-inherent Body of Christendom. Their separate and individual love of the Lord, so far a wholly and merely personal thing, is being changed into that *shared love* which flows through and unites the whole Body. The individual's experience of 'falling in love' with the Lord is now being changed (indeed 'transubstantiated' would seem to be the only possible word) into that divine *caritas* which co-inheres in all the members, binding them all to each other and all to the Lord, and which out of a collection of odd individuals has made the Living Body of the Church.

But the separate Apostles became the Church only by losing the visibility of the vision which originally called them. It seems strange that we have never realised this with all our talk about the Ascension being the 'last of the Resurrection appearances'. It was indeed the last, and the very absence of any further appearances to the individuals forged them into a new wholeness of being. For the Apostles the vision of glory of the Risen Lord was first seen, then lost, then transmuted. Maybe this is the only way by which weak and limited human nature ever can come to such a transformation of being either in religion or in love. May it not be precisely the same for romantic lovers: that they will be turned into a co-inherent whole only by their loss, and by what they make out of it? There are individualist Christians who attack the Church for its institutionalism. There are lovers who attack the institutionalism of marriage. Both institutions have their dangers, but we may question whether without either institution the original love could ever come to that enlargement which is at once its loss and its fulfilment.

And so, intertwined in this poem with the vision of the Apostles at the Ascension, is the vision of lovers at recognition, the only authority which can work with these two persons. But the two visions are not separated, they are deliberately joined, and this is the daring note of the poem. 'Flickered his presence in your

hair.' Few love poets before have dared to go so far,
but we know now something of what this means and
of its essential truth. And then, like the Spirit Who
was to lead the Church into all truth, come the vows
and pledges of marriage, the institution which is to
hold them. These and the continued remembrance
of what was.

> All things he shall in order due
> Bring to remembrance; he
> Infallibly shall hold us true
> And indefectibly.

That is marriage, the institution, that still remembers
its origin. But those in the 'quarry-sweating stage' can
scarcely be expected to understand. 'Incredible is this
to prove?' they ask; and the answer calls them back to
what they knew once long ago. 'Ah, how incredible was
Love!' Even though the vision be gone, yet 'we know
in whom we have believed'. So the Apostles knew;
so lovers too must know. 'Our Church her mission
hath received'; and 'Church' here surely has a double
meaning: it means the body of Christian believers on
the one hand and the pledged couple on the other.
And in each case the mission is the same: to turn the
romantic love of the individual into 'Christendom'.
On the one hand the Mystical Body of Christ made out
of all those living by the *caritas* of the grace of Christ;
on the other the bi-unity of two persons united to each
other (and eventually to all men?) by the same *caritas*
which grows out of their willed servitude and substitution. In each case the pattern is the same; it comes by
loss and withdrawal.

Now the first thing to ask about a poem such as this is: does it correspond to reality? That the one strand, that of the experience of the Apostles, is true, would be agreed upon by all who hold the historic faith of Christendom. They believe that it did in fact work out in this manner. But is the other strand true, and are they in fact so closely allied, so intertwined, as he suggests? We can at any rate never pretend that such questions have not been asked; nor that one great Christian poet and thinker has not answered in the affirmative. Future ages may perhaps find a different answer to the question, but they will at the least have to incorporate these ideas into any final solution. And if there be any truth at all in these suggestions, then they can surely shed a flood of light upon one of the most difficult problems of married life, and one that troubles thousands of bewildered lovers.

But there is a much more important question which, in this modern world at least, has to be faced. Supposing that these ideas are true, then what do they mean, what indeed can they mean, for those who know little or nothing of the Life of the Incarnate God and of His Body the Church? What validity have they for such people?

Surely this: that however little they may know of the theory of the pattern, they can, and often do if they are sincere, work the same pattern out in practice. (Not that a knowledge of the theory might not help a great many of them to avoid near-disaster.) Surely two people, however secular-minded and lacking in formal religion they may be, *if* they have had a valid recognition, and if they have not fallen into the Devil's traps (or if, having fallen, they have recovered the right road later on) can, if they attempt sincerely to follow out what they have seen, achieve two things. First of all, if they keep faith with the vision they have seen, submit to the authority of their first love and keep their pledges in times of withdrawal, then they must, by the very self-sacrifice and living in each other that is needed for this, be already turning their romantic love into at least the beginnings of what the theologians call *caritas*. However little conscious such people may be of the divine origin of the pattern, they may yet be living after the manner of the pattern. They will therefore in fact be making the same grand experiment which the devout make with greater knowledge: but not necessarily with any greater success.

And secondly, such people will learn many things by the hard road of experience. They will discover that love always means both joy and sacrifice; that such sacrifice is always vicarious and therefore effective in another; that in the end there is no healing to be found anywhere save in what we called 'the house of another'. Thus however much they may despise the official Church, they will be following her doctrine of substitution and co-inherence in another. They will find the practical truth of the saying that 'he that loseth his life shall find it'; and only he. And thus, however misguided their thoughts on religion may be, they will be finding out, in their own perhaps bitter experience, some of those truths which the Faith proclaims as being of the very pattern of reality. They may not as yet recognise love as coming from God, but they will have learnt that love (*caritas* now) does in fact rule all. Dante once called love a 'Lord of terrible aspect', and this is what they may be finding out. And he may lead them to that other Lord of terrible aspect whose name is God.

It is the eternal cry of the world that the Christian faith seems so often to have little or no connection with daily life, with that 'cloud of days' which presses upon us all. But here surely it is daily life, often in its most troublesome and boring side, which can be seen as being the faith and the pattern in action.

IX

BRIEF ENCOUNTER

You made me love you; I didn't want to do it.
Popular song of World War I.

MARRIAGE can be wrecked not only by sin and selfishness; it may be wrecked just as easily by lack of knowledge. While many marriages come to a sad end because one or other of the couple was too selfish or too thoughtless to care what happened, there are others that go on the rocks because the bewildered people just did not know what was happening to them. The sea of matrimony is not easy to chart; the pattern has some very unexpected turns. One of these we have already studied under the name of 'withdrawal': the disappearance of the vision, not through death or physical removal, but through what seems to be a perfectly natural and unavoidable fading out. A disappearance that is either temporary, or, in extreme cases, permanent; but which in either case seems to be as unexpected as it is unwanted.

But there is a second phenomenon which is perhaps even more disconcerting. This is not the disappearance of the vision, but its reappearance: but reappearance this time through the person of someone else.

This is a disturbing thing to happen; and even the deepest love does not seem able to prevent it. It certainly happened to Dante, for there is no other explanation of that strange person whom he calls the Lady of the Window. Indeed, if this lady be not Gemma Donati, his wife, then it looks as if this happened to him more than once. Now Dante specifically tells us that, when looking at the Lady of the Window, he experienced the same *stupor*—'shifting of apprehension' is what we called it—that he had experienced on first seeing Beatrice. Rather naturally, perhaps, he thought that such a feeling was a kind of treachery to Beatrice, and he tried to put it from him. But he found he just could not do it, and, in the end, he was forced to admit that love, 'the Lord of terrible aspect', was speaking to him through the Lady of the Window just as truly as he had once spoken through Beatrice. However awful to contemplate, apparently it just was so—as so often it is: and we have to find an explanation.

Dante, not being married to Beatrice, was saved from the worst qualms and complications; but what happens to those who are married? C. S. Lewis calls it a 'troublesome phenomenon', and this is indeed putting it mildly.

Every married man knows that there are times when he cannot help recalling, often with a kind of nostalgia, the calf-loves and the prophets of older days. Many people, especially when their marriage is in the 'quarry-sweating stage', are troubled by the haunting memory of those whom they loved in youth but did not marry. Those they had loved and then forgotten: but did they really forget? or is not the very forgetfulness felt to be a sort of treachery?

But this is something far worse, this Lady of the Window. For here is love, love in its full meaning, seeming to appear after marriage in the form of a romantic recognition of another, a different person. We know there are reasons enough, psychological and others, why middle-aged men and women tend to fall into sentimental infatuations. But these are merely the aberrations of those who feel that their youth is flying, and they can be dealt with easily enough when diagnosed. It is the other thing, the apparently genuine article, which is so frightening. And it does happen. It has perhaps never been more accurately or sympathetically described than in Noel Coward's film *Brief Encounter*.

This is a perfect description and, whether brief or not, it is an encounter into which any of us may fall. It is deeply disturbing. That original vision of recognition which preceded marriage was, so one had come to believe, absolutely unique; something had been seen and recognised which belonged (or so it seemed) absolutely and uniquely to the beloved. Of course it had faded to some extent, but that was only to be expected, that was just the way of the world. We might regret the fading, but we could at least accept it as part of the pattern. But that the same vision should suddenly reappear in the face and form of someone else: that is the terrifying, the inexplicable thing.

Yet if it does happen, then it must somehow be worked into the pattern. If love does these queer things to us, then an explanation must lie somewhere within the pattern of love itself. Can we find this? The first thing to do is probably to make the frank acknowledgement that no one can ever help such a thing happening to him. To that extent the modern world is right when it calls love by the name of that 'fate' from which, when it strikes, no man may escape. No one can ever help it happening; but they can always help what they do about it. Jean Guitton pointed to these twin truths when he said, of a man caught in just such an encounter: 'The expression of his love can be prevented; but he cannot prevent himself from loving'.[1] This of course is where Mother Kirk's usual advice, and the even less-thought-out conventions that derive from her teaching, have so completely missed the mark. An experience like this may well be, indeed certainly will be, a temptation to sin; but to call something which we cannot help a sin in itself is just silly. To tell people who are caught in the toils of such an encounter that it is all imagination and delusion is neither accurate nor kind. For in some cases at least, imagination is just what it is not. Nor is it ever kind to encourage people to refuse to face reality. This thing has happened, and it has a genuine reality; that must be our starting-point. To make such an admission may well be the first step towards getting the world to listen to what we have to say, for the world is always falling into these brief encounters. It knows their power and their terror too well ever to attempt to deny them.

Such affairs do happen; but why? What is the explanation, and what can people be expected to do

[1] *Essay on Human Love*, p. 123.

when they fall headlong into such an experience? We have already hinted at the answer in the hesitant terms in which (in the light of our fuller knowledge) we re-described the original crisis: 'was, so one had come to believe, absolutely unique'; 'something . . . belonged (or so it seemed) absolutely . . . to the beloved'. We may recall that it was one of the Devil's traps to imagine that the vision was personal to the beloved; and that the whole purpose of the grand experiment was to show us that such an idea is in fact the reverse of truth. Those who are 'adult in love' have learned, or should have learned, that the vision does not belong to the beloved but the beloved belongs to the vision. Something universal was then seen in and through one person. That is true enough; but, though seen in and through one person only, it still remains something universal; and a state of perfect *caritas* would, we said, enable us to see this universal thing in all people. May we not suppose, therefore, that, in the approach to that state, we may at times see and recognise a particular person as belonging to this universal vision? Why not indeed—in theory? The real trouble is that this is not just a nice and tidy philosophical theory; it is something experienced in a storm of emotion. And the storm of emotion is exactly similar to that other one which accompanied the recognition that led to the marriage. It is probably this similarity of feeling, more than anything else, that knocks people off their balance and prevents them from being able to consider the situation with the calmness which it needs.

But there is another consideration to which we may

M

turn for guidance, one that is based upon normal human psychology. It is the theory to which Dr. Sherwin Bailey has given the name of 'acceptable variants'. His starting-point might well be another sentence of Jean Guitton's: 'The crisis can indeed recommence with another subject, but then it is only an imitation which takes its mode and colour from the first event. If one loves truly several times, it is without doubt by a repetition.' [1] Is this the explanation of the false prophet, of why the real vision always recalls, and sometimes rather uncomfortably, the one who went before? But Dr. Bailey would go considerably further than this. To put it briefly, what he suggests is that each one of us forms, in the depths of his or her sub-conscious, an ideal picture or figure of the partner of the opposite sex; a picture of the person who would, for us, incarnate the ideal complementary or 'better half'. It is the dimly glimpsed figure of that other half with whom we could make the wholeness that is the image of God in Man. For each of us then this 'dream-figure' (though not conscious enough even to appear in dreams, except perhaps in first adolescence) will possess certain qualities and characteristics, physical, mental and spiritual. But the two important things to remember about this ideal are, first that it is unconscious, and second that, being an ideal of per-fection, it never actually exists anywhere at all. Never-theless we are always in search of him or her. Like the 'dance-hall teenager looking for Mr. Right' we spend a large part of our youth at least in a frantic search for one whom, when he or she appears, we are

[1] *Essay on Human Love*, p. 64.

certain we shall recognise. This is precisely what we do, for that is what falling in love is. It is recognising a particular person as 'being' this dream-figure. Not of course the literal dream-figure, who nowhere exists, but another of the same compelling species. What in fact the scientists would call a 'variant' of the species, but a sufficiently close variant to be 'acceptable' to us. This is another and an equally true meaning which can be given to that word 'recognition', which we have used all along to describe the same crisis. But because this dream-figure was wholly unconscious, the recognition of its variant produces an emotional storm of considerable violence. It cannot help doing so as the subconscious rushes up into actuality.

So far so good; we find an acceptable variant, and marriage may or may not follow. If it does not follow, then we know that we must hope to meet another acceptable variant who may one day light on our path and strike us with just the same feeling of inevitability and uniqueness. (It is strange, by the way, that this experience of making a second recognition does not trouble us; it is only 'brief encounter' under safer circumstances. It surely also disposes of the illusion of 'uniqueness.) There must be very many men and women who did not marry their first love, but met a later acceptable variant with whom they made a very happy marriage. But that means that such people have so far met at least two acceptable variants. We must now introduce another term and say that once we have married the first, or a subsequent, variant, then that particular one has now become for us the *accepted* variant. He or she is now the accepted variant with whom the grand experiment is actually being worked out.

But does this give us any reason to suppose that we may not encounter other acceptable variants later on in life? After all, most of us met one, or perhaps even more, before the one who became the accepted. Now there seems to be nothing at all in theory to deny, and everything in practice to suggest, that such encounters are extremely common: so common in fact that they might almost be said to be a normal part of the pattern of love, something which everyone might expect to have to encounter.

But if such an encounter should occur, we must realise that it will be accompanied by just the same kind of crisis of recognition as occurred with the one that led to marriage. Its emotional accompaniment will be equally shattering. Indeed there are two very good reasons why it may at least appear to be even more disturbing. We said in the previous chapter that such brief encounters have a fatal, but not unnatural, habit of turning up just when marriage to the already accepted variant has reached the dullness of the 'withdrawal' stage. The contrast between the two variants will then be particularly glaring; and all the petty domestic circumstances, and personal irritations, that are inseparable from close living together will only add more fuel to the flames. That is one reason: there is also at work an even more powerful one. Since the accepted variant is not the ideal or perfection, then he or she must inevitably lack some of the qualities of the complete dream-figure. But if the newly seen acceptable variant happens to possess just those qualities, then the encounter will be particularly shattering. These limitations in the present partner have been put up with, their absence has been accepted. But these missing qualities have always been subconsciously desired, and now they appear with dazzling clarity in someone else.

Now all we have said about recognition, and the real and inner meaning of the vision then seen, is true of *all* recognitions; it is something that belongs to the experience itself, no matter under what circumstances it may strike or through what person it may be seen. This fresh recognition is then in itself a vision, an 'image'; that is, an experience of good. On the other hand, illicit love-affairs and adulteries (and, for those who follow Mother Kirk strictly, divorces too) are always experiences of evil. Our trouble is that, lured on by the false romanticism and heady sentimentalism of our age, we inevitably tend to turn the one into the other. But need we do so? Need the fact that all are tempted to turn the good into the bad, and that many actually do so, alter the primal fact that, as we have just said, any recognition is, by itself and of its own very nature, meant to be an experience of beatitude? This recognition too is meant to be so, just as truly as were all the others.

There are in fact two mistakes, two traps of the Devil, by the avoidance of which we may come to the real heart of the matter. The first, perhaps natural, mistake is to imagine that the new acceptable variant is himself or herself perfection. The fact that the already accepted variant now shows all the marks of an extremely limited human being only reinforces this

false idea. The accepted variant is certainly not perfection, and by now we see this only too clearly. But
neither were any variants of the past; nor is this new
one. The practical advice to be given to people in such
a case is then quite simple. Instead of saying 'snap
out of this, it's all imagination', which will in any case
only increase their obstinacy, how much better to say
something like this: 'You must recognise what has
happened to you for what it really is. You have merely
met another acceptable variant. This one is no more
perfection than the one you have already got. And,
since you are already tied to your present variant by
pledges and vows, to say nothing of the subtler bands
forged by long years together, you ought not to do
anything about it. If you do make a change of partners, not only is that wrong and going to cause immense harm to many people, but it may be fraught
with considerable danger. All too soon the new love
will also be seen to be merely human: to be in fact
what she is, only another variant.' And in spite of all
that can be said about the happiness of many second
marriages, this remains severely practical advice.

Dare we suggest that Dante would have been all in
favour of recognising the reality of a second, or even
of a third or fourth, recognition, provided that it did
not hinder or break up the progress of the grand
experiment already in being? If and when the Church
can learn to speak like this, the world may perhaps
listen to her more respectfully than it has done in the
past. That is something to be hoped for; for if the
world will listen when we say this, it may go further
and listen when we say something else: something

which is equally true, but not nearly so attractive. For, having admitted all this, we must at once go on to add that recognition by itself does not give any claims. Claims, pledges, vows, fidelity, all that we mean by the word 'absolute': these belong by right to the already undertaken grand experiment with the already accepted variant. Otherwise we should be back again with the idea of 'the kingdom for the king', instead of the necessary reversal of that idea which is part of God's order. Claims and the absolute are always on the side of the accepted: who, we must never forget, was once an acceptable variant recognised through crisis.

To avoid the second mistake, we have however to accept that reversal of appearances which was the true, but then hidden, meaning of the original vision. We have to realise that the unique is, in one sense at least, not unique after all. That which was glimpsed in the original crisis of the vision of recognition undoubtedly seemed unique, but in reality it was not. It is the whole matter of the grand experiment (whether normally by marriage, or through the 'death of Beatrice') to bring us to a state when we can at least realise this. Recognition was the vision, at that time through one person only, of what all men truly are in the Mind of God. To see this in full, to see all men like this, is of course what the Church means by Beatitude or Heaven—or rather it is the consequence of really seeing God. But if the vision of romantic love was 'the first preparatory form' of beatitude, possible to us at that time only through one person, then that person has really thereby ceased to be unique. This final and complete vision in Heaven will, we presume (rightly? one is not quite sure), be free from emotional accompaniments, certainly from emotional entanglements. And in our brief encounters it is of course the emotional entanglements of all three persons which cause the trouble.

· Charles Williams has some wise words on this subject: 'It may be well enough for those who do not believe in the objective reality of the glory to be content with their chance sensations, to be pseudo-romantically discriminatory towards one, or pseudo-romantically indiscriminatory towards all. The first is ideal sentimentalism, the second is ideal promiscuity.' [1] It is typical of Williams' curiously individual approach to the whole subject that he can seriously use a phrase like 'ideal promiscuity'; as it is the measure of the obtuseness of many conventionally instructed Christians that they will certainly be unable to understand it. But there will, on the other hand, be many who, while condemning promiscuity, however 'ideal', will shrink from any condemnation of sentimentalism. To be sentimental towards the one particular person to the exclusion of all others, is widely assumed to be the proper thing. But is it so in fact? Has the pattern of love that comes from 'the Lord of terrible aspect' much place for sentimentalism? The grand experiment is certainly not to be built on sentimentalism alone, as every married couple discovers as soon as the honeymoon is over, if not before. Nor can the vision of others as God sees them ever come to eyes clouded over with sugary sentiment. This true vision of all humanity as caught up in the final

[1] *The Figure of Beatrice*, p. 47.

pattern of Divine Love must not be allowed to be
obscured by any too sentimental attachment to one
alone. Having said this, one must at once add that
there is the reverse danger: that of losing the vision
altogether through neglect to 'affirm' the one. The
true balance is indeed a knife-edge, and the pattern
has the finest of dividing-lines in it.

Yet the second recognition or 'image' is not to be
denied, nor any possible third either. For love, if it be
genuine love, is always something from God; it is
always an 'image' that has a place somewhere in the
pattern of glory. The fact that most of us may want
to drag it out of its proper place does not deny that it
has its place. Again we are at one with the modern
world which insists upon the reality of this second love;
as we are poles apart from it when we deny that even
love is absolute in itself. There is no absolute save God
Himself, God Who is mirrored in many images and in
many ways that are of His own strange devising. No,
the second 'image' is not to be denied, and yet: 'The
physical union which is permitted, encouraged, and
indeed made part of the full *salute* of that first experience, is to be forbidden to any other.'[1] But why,
asks the world, should it be forbidden, when the vision
is not only credible, but also apparently identical?
There are all sorts of practical reasons which forbid
those threats to the institution of marriage which brief
encounters always carry with them: the stability of
home and family life; the security of children; the
importance of pledges, of loyalty and the keeping of
promises solemnly made. But we must go a good deal

[1] Id., p. 49.

deeper than just these (important and vital though they are) if we are to succeed in finding a place for these brief encounters in the pattern of love, and are at the same time to deny them their 'natural' consummation. What, we must ask over again, was the real purpose of that recognition which led to marriage, as distinct from the natural desires which accompanied it? It was, as we have seen, the formation of 'wholeness', or 'twy-nature', of that bi-unity which is humanity's chief glory and the reflection of God. And secondly, it was the following of the way to God through the affirmation of an image. But, as in all affirmations of any image on the true path to God, 'the aim of the Romantic Way is the two great ends of Liberty and Power'.[1] Precisely; and in order to be truly free, one must have the power both to accept and to reject, to take and not to take. Otherwise freedom does not lie in us but in that which forces us either to take or to reject. To exercise this power of choice one must be given opportunities both of taking and also of rejecting, however little one may relish the latter. Real freedom is, in the final count, identical with willed servitude, for it means freedom and power to respond to the pattern one has accepted. Real freedom, that is, responds to the pattern itself rather than to one's own conception of it. It does the exact opposite of moulding the world 'nearer to the heart's desire'. Power and Liberty alike are learnt by refusing as well as by taking.

As to why God should have willed, as the Church firmly believes that He has, that the pattern should

[1] *The Figure of Beatrice*, p. 49.

involve physical union being kept exclusively for the lifelong adventure of the grand experiment, that is another matter, and one for which we have already suggested several reasons. Let us add that this limitation of coitus to one grand experiment (and therefore to only one of several recognitions that may occur) does not in any way make light of the importance, or of the holy gravity and joy of this act. Rather is it meant precisely to magnify and glorify the importance of the relationship which has this act as its full *salute*. And also to make real and manifest the glory of two persons thus entwined in a bi-unity which is a reflection of the Unimaged Himself.

Once we realise this, and realise also that true freedom comes only by refusing as well as by taking, we can see that, even in spite of the feelings and wishes of the time, any recognition of another image must, after marriage, be worked out in a different mode. 'Consummation' and 'fruition', if we may use such words, may indeed be possibilities, but they must be of a different kind and achieved in a different manner from the normal. We are really being offered the opportunity of serving that love to which we ourselves belong by virtue of the first recognition, in a new and different manner. If only we can rise to the occasion! To quote again: 'Having thriven in one manner, we are offered the opportunity of thriving in another. . . . The second image is not to be denied; we are not to pretend it is not there, or indeed to diminish its worth; we are only asked to free ourselves from concupiscence in regard to it.'[1] (Just as, presumably, in affirming the

[1] Id., p. 49.

first image we had to free ourselves from the concupiscence of the demon jealousy; for jealousy is just
spiritual concupiscence and has probably caused far
more harm than has adultery. If only the Church had
thundered against the former with half the indignation
which she has hurled at the latter!) 'Only asked to
free ourselves of concupiscence': it sounds so little, yet
it will take all that most of us have. The first image,
or rather the image whose recognition led to the acceptance of that variant, is one towards physical
union. That is because the pattern of all recognitions
leads, in emotional and physical feeling, to a desire
for physical union. It is this desire of *all* recognitions
for physical union, and the limitation of physical
union to *one* recognition, which at last puts physical
union in its proper place within the whole pattern of
love. Physical union is an 'image within an image',
a diagram within the larger pattern. As such, and in
its own proper place, it is a constituent of the glory.
But this means also that in any recognition we shall
feel the same desire, whatever in fact we do about it.
Such feelings are a natural part of the act of recognition itself. But the true pattern says that in this second
recognition we are being directed towards something
else, something which is also itself a part of the
pattern: that is, towards the power and freedom which
come from refusal. The 'image within an image' must
now be towards separation, not union: separation in
reality and in will, for our feelings will inevitably be
something different. And yet, whatever our feelings
at the moment of torment, we have to realise that both
the first and the second image, both the acceptance of

the one and the refusal of the other, are 'alike intense towards most noble Love; that is, towards the work of the primal Love in the creation'.[1]

No one is likely to suggest that such a solution will be an easy one. Yet it would be difficult to suggest any other solution which could do justice to the two things which we are forced to recognise as being parts of the given pattern of love. These are, on the one hand, the order which the Church believes has come from God and, on the other hand, the reality of romantic love. We must accept the fact that the 'proper' and divinely intended way towards the sexual fulfilment of humanity lies through monogamous marriage. But we are also forced to realise that 'our most courteous Lord' (Love—or God—or both?) scatters His gifts and His largesse where He wills.

What it really comes down to is this: that the appearance of a second recognition is not meant to be the beginning of a second experiment. Its meaning is rather something different: the prolongation of the first experiment in a different mode. And this is to be done by 'a preference of the principle of satisfaction to satisfaction itself'.[2] This also would seem to be a tall order for most people; yet all that we have said about the necessary affirmation of loss and limitation, of freedom through refusal, can scarcely be learnt without something very like it.

Towards the end of that remarkable chapter in *The Figure of Beatrice* from which these quotations are taken

[1] *The Figure of Beatrice*, p. 49.
[2] Id., p. 51.

there occurs this passage: 'If it were possible to create in marriage a mutual adoration towards the second image, whenever and however it came, and also a mutual limitation of the method of it, I do not know what new liberties and powers might not be achieved.'[1] Put in plain language, this would seem to mean that all three persons in the triangle of a brief encounter should face and understand the reality of what has happened, and should then continue in harmony and in mutual three-sided friendship. It could not easily be done, and, for normal weak humanity, would seem to be rather dangerous advice. But before condemning such an idea out of hand we had better read Maude Royden-Shaw's book *A Threefold Cord*. In that book we see something very like this actually happening: an encounter between two persons, one of whom was already married. But this was an encounter that was anything but brief, and one in which, instead of the usual 'eternal triangle' of fiction and its disasters, we find a cementing friendship of the three which was undoubtedly a threefold cord of liberty and power for all three. There are many who could not rise to this; but for those who can, what strange opportunities may not lie in wait!

After this it need scarcely surprise us to discover that it is in his treatment of the 'second image' that Williams has been most fiercely attacked, and notably by Father H. D. Hanshell in an article published in *The Month* for January 1953. It may be, as Father Hanshell suggests, that Williams has misinterpreted Dante on the matter. Only a Dante scholar can put us

[1] *The Figure of Beatrice*, p. 50.

right about that. But, leaving that aside, the whole manner in which Father Hanshell abruptly dismisses the second image ('married persons, for example, will know how to deal with the second image should it occur') is a perfect example of the reasons why the world simply refuses to listen to Mother Kirk. Not only are there, alas! many quite serious married couples who do not know how to deal with it, and wish to heaven that they did; but Father Hanshell puts this whole sentence in parentheses, thus suggesting that to him it is of no importance and can be dismissed with a shrug. But it cannot be so easily dismissed; theology has got to deal with it somehow. Father Hanshell would probably question the orthodoxy of Williams' theology (and on grounds which may themselves be questioned), but it is surely one of the most hopeful signs of the times that a theologian of Williams' stature should have taken the matter so desperately seriously. He faced a world which he knew, by the insight of both a poet and a lover, was being driven to desperation by just such encounters, and he propounded a possible solution. That is something of which account must now always be taken.

For the truth is that 'brief encounter', like everything else in the complicated pattern of love and marriage, is not something which can ever be looked at in isolation. The whole purpose of the Way of Affirmation, as of the Way of Rejection for those called to it, is to widen and deepen one's love. We are to be led from 'love' (in one mode) of one person, to 'love' (in a different but equally real mode) of others: eventually, of course, to 'love' of all. As the preachers are never tired of telling us, this enlarged love, or *caritas*, must include those persons whom we happen to dislike. (It may perhaps be even easier to practise it towards them than towards those whom we like too much!) But surely it must also include any acceptable variants whom we may happen to meet. Indeed such persons, by their very closeness to our own nature and their inevitable involvement with us, should have a very special place in that pattern of love which has been laid upon us. Might it not be said that these troublesome 'brief encounters' are meant to be the opportunities which are offered, to those who can take them, of practising this disinterested love as the pattern unfolds and as we go further along the way?

'To those who can take them.' It seems unfortunately to be the case that such opportunities are offered just as frequently to those who are incapable of taking them as to those who are, or who might be. But that again may be merely 'one of Allah's little games': or that very largesse with which our courteous Lord scatters His gifts to all and sundry.

This is not exactly a pleasant thought. But then a good deal in both the Christian religion and in the practice of real and genuine love is not pleasant at first sight. The truth may be that 'brief encounters', like 'withdrawal' itself, are sent or allowed us as opportunities of learning to see all men as God sees them.

We need not be expected to like them any the more for that; but maybe we ought to learn to welcome them when they arrive.

X

LARGESSE

And so they are now living in a state of happy sin.
(Despairing report of a Moral Welfare Worker)

WE have discovered by this time that the pattern of
love is by no means the simple thing which it appeared
to be in the first blaze of glory. In this life we can do
nothing, and especially nothing which involves an
encounter with another person, without taking risks.
We have now gone through some of the dangers of
the romantic way, some of the risks which are inevitably involved in any real attempt both to discover
and to follow the pattern of love.

First of all there were the dangers and traps inherent
in the very nature of the recognition crisis itself. Then
there were the dangers that come from the slow, hard,
and often grinding day-to-day life of any two persons
involved in such a high mutual adventure as the
making of the grand experiment. And, lastly, we
faced that part of the pattern which may involve the
reappearance of the vision in the face of another. To
all of these we attempted some kind of explanation and
solution.

All these are personal problems which have to be

N

faced by those who have been suddenly, and often almost against their will, pitchforked into love, and so forced to discover and work out the pattern. This they do in varying ways and with varying success. But because their ways vary and because, to them, the pattern is often obscured and clouded over by the mists of sentiment or self-interest, there arises one more problem which is to-day of vital and desperate importance. It is a practical problem certainly, but its importance for us arises out of that very nature and high purpose which we have said lies behind the whole experience of love.

What we have aimed so far at proving is that romantic love and a real attempt at following the Way of Affirmation in the grand experiment of marriage can and do, in innumerable cases of happy marriage—and in many only 'moderately successful' ones also—, succeed in producing something which we have tried to describe in such terms as 'wholeness', 'bi-unity', or a 'twy-nature'. In very varying degrees will different couples succeed in making this thing for which the pattern exists. But most of them will come some way at any rate along the road which both makes for wholeness and transforms romantic love into something wider and deeper. Most of them will build something which can be seen and known, and which bears some resemblance to that thing which God meant love to create.

But, having said this, we are, if we are honest, forced to admit that such an apparent 'wholeness out of mixture', such a real co-inherence and bi-unity of purpose and of person, can sometimes be found outside the bonds of matrimony. It can be found, and we all know it, in many couples who have never been through a wedding ceremony of any kind, but who yet are living happily and faithfully together. Very often it is to be found in those cases which probably bother Mother Kirk even more, the secular second marriages of divorced persons: marriages which, according to her, ought not to exist at all. In an earlier chapter we made reference to Alaric Jacob's *Scenes from a Bourgeois Life*, and quoted what he said about the false prophet who so often goes before real love.[1] He married Miranda, and there are subsequent passages which describe for us something of the joy and the happiness which came to him from that marriage: joys which he calls, as any true lover would, utterly undeserved. No one can read these passages unmoved, nor doubt that he is describing something deep and lasting. Yet Miranda had, as he tells us, already been divorced when he married her.

Now this is precisely the kind of thing from which Mother Kirk has shied away with all the terror of a nineteenth-century horse facing its first motor-car. But the car is there; it cannot be ignored. Such things are not illusions, and until we have some real explanation, and moreover one that will do justice to the binding nature of such unions as felt by the persons concerned, we have not probed fully into the mysteries and vagaries of love. Nor shall we have anything to say to which the world will listen for a moment. Somehow we have got to fit these things into the complexity of the full pattern of love.

[1] p. 71.

To put it shortly, the problem appears to be this: there are couples who seem to produce the results of the grand experiment (or at least some of the results) under conditions which we are already agreed ought not to be used for that experiment. Some, for instance, have made out of that 'brief encounter' a second experiment; though, as we have just seen, that was not its purpose at all.

This is of course no new problem. No less a person than the great St. Augustine found himself dealing with something very similar in the fourth century. He too had to face the fact that there were couples living together faithfully and loyally, and presumably bringing up their children in a proper manner, who yet had never been married to each other. What, he asks, can we call their union? is it merely a sinful liaison? No one can imagine that he looked with favour upon affairs like these, and we can see how it must have gone against the grain to say what he did about them. For he says quite definitely that if such persons intend to remain exclusively faithful to each other till death, and if they raise a family, then 'not without reason' can their union 'be called marriage'. Of the three things which he says are the essence of marriage they possess two, faithfulness and offspring; and since these completely differentiate their union from a casually lustful affair, he will not deny to it the name of marriage.[1] St. Augustine was talking of marriage and not of love, but that is only natural because, as we believe, the whole business of romantic love, and its acceptance as part of the normal pattern of life, was still some

[1] *De Bono Conjugali*, 5: 5.

seven hundred years in the future. Not that the thing
itself did not exist in some cases; and indeed St.
Augustine may well have known it in his own life:
known it and cast it from him—dare one say in a
partial misunderstanding of its real nature? We might
even go further and suggest that it was the very
memory of his own heart-breaking experience which
made him so unexpectedly tender and charitable in his
judgements of such uncanonical unions? The problem
of the re-married divorcee did not exist for him.

However, we must face the fact that it seems possible for some people to make the grand experiment
without that form or institution which we say is necessary and proper for it. Doubtless they ought not to do
so, but they do. There are therefore two questions
that arise. First the question whether this is really a
grand experiment after all; whether that which it
seems to produce is that real wholeness and 'twy-
nature' (we are now approaching dangerously near to
the theological term *henosis*) or not. And secondly, if
it is genuinely the grand experiment, how important
is that phrase we used: '*ought not* to do so'.

There are two possible answers to the first question;
and though they do not provide anything like a full
solution of the problem, they must be mentioned
because they probably apply to quite a number of
cases. The first is the suggestion that things which
look exactly alike may in reality be quite different, or
at least may proceed from quite different underlying
causes. Those who have read C. S. Lewis' little
pamphlet *Transposition* may remember the two instances of this which he gives and his suggested

explanation. The first instance is the passage in Pepys's Diary where the author says that listening to certain music had such a powerful effect upon his soul that it made him feel physically sick. The other instance is an attempted explanation, in the light of what Pepys had said, of the 'speaking with tongues' at Pentecost. The critics are for ever telling us that *glossolalia* is a well-known phenomenon of psychological hysteria. Professor Lewis neatly turns the edge of this by accepting it as a fact on the natural plane. But, says he, Pepys's nausea was equally a fact on the natural plane. Only this time it was produced, not by indigestion nor by too much drink, but by something else. But why should music do this? Because the human frame is so limited that there are only a few sensations which are capable of being used to suggest anything at all. There was in fact no other vehicle of expression in the limited human frame of Pepys which the emotion of uplift caused by the music could use. Hence the nausea. So, he argues, there was no other vehicle or sensation or effect on the personality which the Holy Ghost could use except psychological hysteria. But what looked on the surface like mere nausea or cheap-jack hysteria, what in a million normal cases would be just these and nothing more, was, in these two exceptional cases, really the outcome of something very different. The spirit of music in the one case and the Holy Spirit of God in the other.

There is no answer to a suggestion like this; the negative cannot be proved. But it does suggest to us that we should not say that things which look exactly alike are always really alike. After all, both calf-love and infatuation often look like a genuine romantic recognition. It would be dangerous to press this analogy too far perhaps, but it ought not to be ignored altogether.

The other possible answer might be illustrated by a picture of two motor-cars racing each other along two exactly parallel roads. One road is of infinite length, while the other is comparatively short. Obviously the car on the longer road could go very much farther than the other one could. But equally obviously what will really happen depends entirely upon the two drivers. If the driver on the short road is a speed-fanatic, while the other is lazy and easy-going, it follows that within a limited time the man on the shorter road might find himself miles in advance of the other. The man on the longer road could go very much farther; but in fact, in the time allowed, he has not got nearly so far. Now every lifetime is limited. May it not then be that there are couples united by no religious ceremony who, in their lifetime, go further along their road, limited though it may be, than many conventionally married couples have ever gone, or even sought to go, along their own road, whose grand infinity they may never even have seen. Even those who would maintain that the shorter road of uncanonical union was utterly and completely separate from the other, must also allow that it runs a parallel course. Any union of persons at all demands unselfishness and self-surrender if it is to come to any success. Anyone with any knowledge of human nature must admit that, on this hypothesis, there are many 'illicit' couples who have gone farther along their parallel course than many most conventional and canonical marriages. But neither of these explanations will cover every case. In the last chapter we suggested that a 'brief encounter' might be unquestionably a real gift of love, but that, if so, it was given us for a different purpose. This gift was offered to us precisely in order that we might make the opposite decision; between acceptance (in the ordinary sense) and refusal. Or rather, that the acceptance of love's gift must mean the rejection of its consummation after that manner which is to be confined to the grand experiment already undertaken. In simpler words: a second love ought to mean rejecting a second union.

But what if we do not do this? What if we cannot do this? What, above all, if we do not know or realise that this is what we are meant to do, and so, in our ignorance, go and tie ourselves up in a second experiment of a forbidden kind? What then?

All that Mother Kirk seems to have done about this so far is to draw her skirts aside and murmur such phrases as: 'It's all wrong'; 'it's all a delusion'. But such murmurings are mere escapism, an attempt to get out of facing the realities of the problem.

Sin has been defined as 'the preference of an immediately satisfying experience of things to the believed pattern of the universe'. It might be put more briefly by calling sin the taking of the short view on a moral issue rather than the long view. That is all very well; but suppose the long view is not known, suppose the particular pattern of the universe which is rejected for a satisfying experience be a pattern which we have never known, or have good reasons for rejecting? This is not a question in the air; apply it to monogamous marriage and the 'for-

bidding' of this second experiment. What if monogamous indissoluble marriage is disbelieved in *ex
animo*? This is quite likely to be the case with many
people to-day. We saw in our first chapter what a
number of people there are who take their opinions
on marriage from the daily newspapers and similar
organs of public opinion which certainly no longer
believe in the absolute or necessary permanence of
marriage. Those who form their opinions thus will not
believe in that 'pattern of the universe' which forbids
the undertaking of a second experiment at every fresh
recognition. (Maybe they ought to have believed in
it. Maybe; but that raises many other problems
besides those of the responsibility or the religion of the
persons concerned.) What are we to say, then, of
those who, when they made this second and uncanonical experiment, did not, could not—as distinct
from would not—believe in the pattern which 'forbade'
it? Surely this is just where the whole business of the
distinction between formal and material sin comes in;
a vital difference which the traditional Church has
always held to most firmly.

What it all really comes to is this; that, while no
man may presume to judge his brother one way or the
other, we must admit that those persons who do not
believe that a certain pattern is laid upon them are not
guilty of formal and deliberate sin if, in good faith,
they go against this pattern. They are breaking the
pattern; we cannot deny that. By breaking it, they
are introducing a fresh jaggedness into the glory that
is meant to be seen in humanity. But if they are not
fully conscious of wrong-doing, then no theologian

worth the name would impute 'guilt' to them person-
ally. And equally, not even the most rigorous theologian would deny the grace of God working in the
lives of such persons—if they seek it. 'They are living
in a state of happy sin' was the remark of a social
worker quoted at the head of this chapter. One knows
the kind of person referred to; one who is unlikely to
have fixed beliefs in patterns of any kind. If (and it is
the 'if' that is crucial) they did not know of the real
pattern, or if for some seemingly good reason they
could not accept it, dare anyone deny that the Spirit
will still give them such grace as they need? And if
that be granted, then surely the Spirit will allow that
some at least of the effects and results of the grand
experiment could appear in their lives. Not only
would they appear, but they would be seen and
noticed as apparently perfectly genuine results. There
are cases indeed in which such genuine results may
put to shame many who ought to have gone much
further along the road of the true pattern, but have
failed to do so.

There is a very remarkable passage in Lady
Pakenham's essay on Marriage which was quoted
earlier, the more remarkable as coming from one who
is a convinced Roman Catholic. Remembering, of
course, that Lady Pakenham is talking about those
who do not accept her Church's teaching on the
indissolubility of marriage, we can see that she is
facing much the same problem, and coming to a
rather similar conclusion:

Most of us can think of people who having made an
unhappy first marriage, after one reshuffle, settle down to

a life of tranquil harmony. Their second marriage seems to extract from them unsuspected qualities of loyalty, tolerance and selflessness totally wanting in the first. One cannot help feeling that nothing but sad precipitateness ruined the first attempt. At the back of the mind was a conviction that 'if things go wrong we can always have another shot'. . . . The precipitateness, of course, is due to the feeling that no precipice exists. But when the moment comes for a second attempt the atmosphere has changed. A broken marriage, even if it was built originally . . . to collapse easily, involves all kinds of unexpected sorrows and discomforts that no one wishes to experience again. . . . So before the second marriage is entered into, the shadow of a precipice has begun to appear. . . . 'It mustn't happen twice' is the feeling now. 'It's going to succeed this time.' And so often it does.[1]

There is the very strong suggestion here that if only the first marriage had been entered into with the seriousness of purpose and the creative effort which marked the second, then very probably the first would also have succeeded. And this is a very powerful argument in the hands of those who have to prepare others for marriage. But it would seem that Lady Pakenham is fully agreed that, if the grace of God is not cut off completely from such persons, by virtue of the fact that they did not know that their second marriage was 'forbidden', then that same grace does undoubtedly allow many of the proper fruits of the grand experiment to appear in such marriages.

It is probable that at this stage we cannot any longer avoid that terrible word of the theologians, *henosis*:

[1] *Catholic Approaches*, pp. 102 f.

that is the 'one-flesh union' spoken of by Christ Himself and by St. Paul. We will presume, and we hope rightly, that this word means that 'twy-nature of wholeness' which ought to be the result of the grand experiment, itself based on the vision of recognition. But here is the dilemma. Mother Kirk says very firmly that no such *henosis* ought to exist outside the confines of her sacramental institution of holy matrimony. She might even seem to say that no such *henosis* can exist outside it, only then she would have St. Augustine to deal with. On the other hand the world, that is ordinary human experience which really does know what appears to happen to men and women, flatly denies this. The world says, with very considerable justification, that something which is, to the outward eye at any rate, quite indistinguishable from *henosis* does exist outside the bonds of indissoluble matrimony. How to resolve the dilemma? Allowing for all that has been said, surely the only possible answer is, literally and accurately, 'God knows'. Not only can we make no accurate judgements on the matter, but we might well follow C. S. Lewis when he said, over another matter, 'our task is precisely not to judge'.

It is possible that there is a clue contained in that word 'sacrament' which was deliberately introduced a few lines above. There are a very large number of Christians who believe that marriage ought indeed to be called by that high and holy name. But no sooner do theologians begin to talk about sacraments than they begin, alas! to dispute about what they call the 'validity' or the 'invalidity' of sacraments.

For those unfamiliar with the disputes of ecclesiastics there is however another connection in which
this word 'valid' has an important meaning, and it is
an illustration that is perhaps even more helpful. It
concerns fighting men in a war. It is, we all realise,
the proper business of a soldier to be courageous and
to fight effectively, as the vast majority of them do.
But twentieth-century warfare has taught us something else. In any large-scale national conflict (and
especially one which involves the horrible process of
occupation of a country by the enemy) there will
to-day always be found not one, but two kinds of
brave and effective fighters. They might perhaps be
called the official and the unofficial. The former com-
prise the officially enlisted or commissioned members
of the State's Armed Forces. The latter are those who
are variously known as the guerrillas, the *francs-
tireurs*, the *maquis*, or the Resistance: and these are
not in uniform. Both bodies contain brave men; both
fight courageously; both may bring about the victory
and liberation of their country. Sometimes indeed
individual members of the unofficial forces may happen to be braver or more effective than some of the
official members; that is purely a matter of personal
character. But between these two bodies there lies one
noticeable and rather terrible difference. It concerns
what will happen should any one of them be captured
alive by the enemy. Uniformed members of the
Armed Forces have the right to be treated as prisoners
of war, and they will probably get honourable treatment. The others will be shot out of hand. Why the
difference? It has nothing whatever to do with either

character or effectiveness. It is simply the result of the fact that, because the regular Forces are in uniform, because their actions are done and authorised by the State itself, they are accepted as a valid part of the pattern of the State at war. The others are not in uniform because their actions have no official part in the pattern of the State. Their actions, though of course widely approved of unofficially, are not officially validated and commissioned by a world-recognised authority. No one will maintain that their actions are any the less effective; in certain cases they may be very much more so. But States at war cannot allow the existence of more than a small number of such people, nor can they ever give official recognition to the highly arbitrary, though useful, actions they commit. Otherwise the whole pattern of the State would be overthrown. The people who join such groups of free fighters must therefore go into it with their eyes open. No one will own them if they are caught. They are, and must remain, completely unofficial and 'invalid'; but they may be extremely effective.

There is a difference, then, between what is called 'valid' and what is effective; and it is here that we can return to the ecclesiastical quarrel over sacraments. Probably by this time everyone realises that the core of the disagreement between the Church of England and the Protestant Churches over the question of Reunion has been narrowed down to the question of the 'validity' of non-episcopal Orders and sacraments. 'Catholics' assert that non-episcopal Orders are 'invalid,' and that the sacraments that flow from them are also 'invalid'. This would certainly seem to be the

view of the official formularies of the Church of
England. The Church of Rome brings exactly the
same charge against the Church of England. Yet
would any Anglican maintain that a Nonconformist
Minister was therefore 'ineffective'? Dare one say
that a Protestant sacrament is 'ineffective'? One is
reminded of the Roman Catholic Abbot who when
questioned about the Sacramental Presence of Christ
in an Anglican church in which the consecrated
elements were reserved, is said to have answered: 'We
cannot say where the Presence is not; we can only say
where It certainly is.' The parallel to the uniformed
soldier and the guerrilla seems to be pretty close. 'Invalid' does not mean the same thing as 'ineffective'.
What 'valid' means is 'within the pattern'. Only those
Orders and sacraments can be considered as 'valid'
which fall within that pattern which—whether rightly
or wrongly does not affect the argument—is believed
to be that which was given by the Holy Spirit to the
Church as a co-inherent and living body. Even the
strictest Roman theology will allow that God's uncovenanted grace may simultaneously accompany an
invalid sacrament (and may therefore render it 'effective' in some degree?).

Now if a sacrament can be invalid (that is, outside
the pattern and order) and yet be effective; if a man
can have all the qualities and effectiveness of a uniformed soldier, and yet be liable to be shot out of hand
because he is not validated by the State; can we not
take the same principle and apply it to the indissolubility of marriage and the conditions that make for
henosis? The Church believes that the divine pattern

for the fulfilment of man's sexual nature is that of indissoluble marriage. This pattern, she believes, has been committed to her both to proclaim and to guard. If the Church has any authority to lay down conditions of life for her own members, if she has any authority to proclaim the Will of God for mankind, then she must make rules and regulations and pronouncements about this particular pattern. She must be able to state clearly and plainly which marital unions are inside this given pattern and which are not; which unions she can validate with the seal of approval and which not. *But of actual effectiveness in the matter of the grand experiment she can say nothing.* She can pronounce no judgement on the effectiveness of any union, whether it be inside the pattern of validity or outside. That is a totally different matter.

It may be that there is a clue here to that dispute which rages among certain religious thinkers: the dispute as to whether Our Lord, when making His stern pronouncements about the indissolubility of marriage, was stating a fact or merely promoting an ideal. The trouble is that to take either side in this debate will land us in serious difficulties. If we say that He was pronouncing a fact, then we shall have to explain away, if we can, all that has been said about what seem to be equally true unions that make their appearance outside marriage. If, on the other hand, we say that He was merely promoting an ideal, then we shall all too soon find ourselves thinking, if not actually saying, that it does not matter so very much if we fall short of this ideal, seeing that we all of us daily fall short of His ideals in so many other ways. In either

case we seem to be slipping away from reality. But
suppose that He was only pronouncing upon the
Divine pattern of validity, without reference to the
effectiveness of any union. Presumably Our Lord, as
God and with the omniscience of God, could pronounce upon the effectiveness of any union, were He
asked. (Indeed, at the Day of Judgement He will do
precisely this; and that is one reason why that Day
will contain so many surprises.) Surely His own remark, 'In the beginning it was not so', implies that it
is the Divine pattern and order about which He is
talking. The Church, if she is to be faithful to the
revelation which she believes He committed to her,
must also make precise statements as to the pattern of
validity. But judgement as to the effectiveness of any
union is perhaps not really her business.

Something like this must have been in the mind of
Charles Williams when he penned that passage in
which he expressed the hope that the official guardians
of religion would keep their hands off the *stupor* of
romantic love. He was sure they would only ruin it.
Then he adds: 'The covenanted mercies are their concern. This, uncovenanted, rides in our very nature
. . . within and without the Church.' [1] Of the uncovenanted mercies it must always be said that they
exist; never must we attempt to deny them. Nor, on
the other hand, dare we ever presume upon them.

Yet perhaps the best word to use in connection with
the strange ways of romantic love is one which we
have already used in connection with God and His
gifts: 'largesse'; 'our courteous Lord's largesse'. It

[1] *The Figure of Beatrice*, p. 188.

o

calls up the picture of the mediaeval lord scattering pieces of gold and silver to the struggling crowd, whereby so many odd people find themselves strangely possessed of something they never expected and probably never deserved. God may not be capricious, but He is certainly unpredictable. And so is love 'the Lord of terrible aspect'. It is a very part of his terror that no one ever knows when or where he will strike. Love, like the wind and the Holy Spirit, 'bloweth where it listeth'.

And yet for the very last word of all we can turn away from the Church and her rigour back to human nature, and we shall find—is it so strange after all?—almost the same thing. Let us think back to those successful second marriages described by Lady Pakenham. How were they made successful? To what do they witness? Surely to that broken and once-betrayed, yet still binding, idea that 'love demands fidelity'. 'Invalid' though they may be, their effectiveness springs entirely from the fact that they are grounded on fidelity. Many people, in their zeal to vindicate the Christian tradition, are led by the present confusion between the doctrines of the Church and the conventions of society to forget a fact of great importance. They overlook the fact that there must be thousands of men, and women too, who are making a brave and uphill fight to remain faithful and loyal to a spouse to whom, according to the Church's rules, they ought not to be united at all. But faithfulness and loyalty and self-sacrifice are always, under any circumstances, a part not only of the largesse given by God to men and women, but also of that largesse

which lovers grant and give to each other. Loyalty
and faithfulness demanded by love and given unstint-
ingly must always be of value.

But these marriages also witness to something else.
They show that human nature at its best knows full
well that love as experienced in the first crisis of recognition is not enough. For such love needs that kind of
permanence out of which alone can grow unity and
wholeness. It deeply desires it at bottom; but it finds
that more than emotion is needed. That is why we
find so often that 'illicit' unions can show something
that more 'licit' ones may lack: fidelity and the will to
permanence. It is not after all so very surprising to
find that there are quite a number of divorced and
re-married couples who 'do not hold with divorce'.
This conviction comes out of their own deep personal
experience, out of what they have known and suffered.
They have now discovered something which they did
not know before: the likeness and diagram of the true
pattern. In their own 'invalid', but by no means
ineffective, way they are striving to work it out afresh.

XI

THE PATTERN OF GLORY

THE word 'pattern' may seem to many to have been used in the last chapter in two different senses, or rather to have referred to two different things. There was of course the sense in which we have been using it all along, that of the pattern of romantic love, recognition, the grand experiment, and so on. But we talked also of the 'pattern of indissolubility' or permanence of marriage as being that pattern which has been given by God in and through which the first one is meant to be worked out. Unless we are careful we shall find ourselves inextricably confused.

Perhaps the best method of working our way through the complication is to consider an actual case and the remarks made about it by one of the persons concerned. If we can analyse the different elements in the story it may help us considerably. As it is a true story we must use fictitious names, and we can start by saying that John met Mary in his youth and was attracted to her. He might perhaps have thought of marriage, but there were many difficulties in the way, and presently Mary passed out of his life. He then married Joan; but this marriage was not based on any crisis of falling in love at all. There was admiration and respect between them, but not apparently much knowledge of real character. The marriage was not a success, though it lasted a good many years; fairly soon John realised that it was not likely to work. At some point during its gradual disintegration John came to the sudden realisation that it was Mary whom he ought to have married. He came suddenly upon that knowledge which we have called recognition. He did not then think that he would ever see Mary again; to his surprise she suddenly reappeared in his life. That proved the breaking-point, and John left his wife and, with her knowledge and at least semi-approval, went and lived with Mary. This uncanonical, and indeed 'uncivil' union (for there was no divorce and legal marriage), lasted for some years until Mary died in middle age. It was however a union that to all appearances, both to John and Mary and to all their friends and acquaintances, was one of very great joy and happiness. It seemed to be the making of a real wholeness out of mixture. The real point, the core of our problem however, lies in the remark which John made when telling the story. He said, 'There was to me far more sin in living with my wife and not loving her at all, than there was in living unmarried with Mary.'

How does this case fit in with either of our patterns? Dare we do, what previously we said that no man can do, make some attempt to apportion the guilt or sin? If John's words were really sincere and spoken from the depths of his conscience, then he may have been innocent of 'formal' sin; but what we have to work out is not so much his personal responsibility as the objective nature of what is involved.

First of all, here is a pattern of love almost as we have been describing it. Here is a union which starts with a recognition, and a long-delayed one too, which goes on to the making of some kind of experiment together, and which shows, so far as the world can see, very fruitful results. If it were not for the complication of that unfortunate original marriage to Joan, it might pass for an almost perfect example. But, whatever its effectiveness, the marriage to Joan made the union with Mary 'invalid'.

But what are we to say about the marriage? Not being based on love it started off 'on the wrong foot', at least for people in our society and with our mental assumptions. However valid it was, it started off under conditions which made any effectiveness extremely precarious and unlikely. Was not the undertaking of such a marriage at all in some sense a sin, whether formal or only material?

But there is more than that, for we must say firmly that such a marriage *could* have endured. Many would say that it ought to have endured, and that the 'enduring of it' was the harder part to which both were really called. 'Some minor by-product', or 'the best of a bad job', could have been made out of it. A following of the true pattern in all its hardness and jaggedness would have demanded this. But it did not happen. Instead, rightly or wrongly, the pattern appeared to have been made in another way.

Surely the first thing to say is that in both unions there was, at least partially, a sin against the true pattern. But equally truly in both unions the pattern was partially followed. Has not then the partial following in *each* case an absolute and independent value of its own? Each did make something; can we not leave it at that?

But if we do, there are some who will say triumphantly that we have all along been making a mistake. They will say that in fact there are two patterns quite separate from each other, a pattern of love and a pattern of marriage, and that the connection between them is really nothing more than fortuitous. This we deny absolutely; it contradicts our whole thesis. But we ought to be able to give some explanation of why things so often look like this.

May it not be another of the effects of the Fall of Man? Whatever the world may say, we can never think theologically without having to come back to the primal fact that there is something wrong with human nature as we know it. There are at least two things which are wrong: we have a disintegrated nature and a divided, or at least inaccurate and troubled, knowledge and judgement. We do not see things—that is, spiritual realities or moral issues—straight, simple and whole. We split and divide them. Is not this just what has happened here? Because of the Fall, Man has split the pattern, split it both in his consciousness and in his experience. There is in fact only one Divine pattern of Love, but our inherent and ineradicable tendency to break everything up and see it askew has split the pattern, or at least distorted it to our view.

This may indeed be so, and from it will flow two

corollaries. The first, which we will deal with later, is that it must henceforth be the task of Redemption to re-unite for us that pattern which the folly and false knowledge of Man has splintered. But the second corollary follows no less inevitably. It is that, though the pattern be thus unnaturally divided both in our thoughts and in our experience, yet each part can still have its own effectiveness. Partial and limited, and therefore perhaps tainted with sin, yet each can be a part of the true pattern. To fail to follow the pattern, either in whole or in part, when one sees and knows what it is, is always sin. But it is equally true that the following of either wing of the splintered pattern can, if its effectiveness be not hindered by conscious wrong-doing, still have its own share of the glory.

Since it is probably the unruliness of our sexual desires which is more responsible than anything else for this splitting of the pattern, it may be as well to have a final look at sex and ask why its power is so strong. If sex be 'an image within an image', a constituent of the glory, why does it trouble us so greatly? Probably for that very reason.

But sex would seem to be in a rather special position. As a mere biological instinct it differs from most of the other biological instincts in one very important particular. The other instincts—for food, drink, shelter and self-defence—are all necessary for the survival of the individual as well as for the survival of the race. But, while the reproductive instinct is just as important and vital for the race as a whole, it is not necessary for any individual ever to put it into explicit action. A man or a woman can live a happy and complete life without allowing the sexual instinct any of its normal functions. Moreover, all sorts of circumstances have arisen in human society which demand that this instinct be at least curbed in all men. Its use must always be limited; and it need not in fact ever be used. But because this instinct is just as necessary for the species, though not for the individual, as are the others, it must remain at least as strong as the others. Hence what troubles mankind is the possession of an instinct that is so strong that only two things can be done about it. It can be mastered by discipline, or wantonly indulged.

But there is in sex, as we have already seen, something far more fundamental than the mere biological urge to prolong the species. There is the whole business of the incompleteness of the individual man and woman, incomplete not just as an individual but as a single-sexed individual. And all this is just as true in ordinary daily life as it is on the high theological plane of the image of God. Men need women, and women need men, and, being made as they are, they instinctively desire the closest and most intimate type of union. None of the ordinary forms of intercourse can satisfy that fundamental longing for completeness in union with the opposite. It might be fairly asked whether a great many unchaste men do not consort with women for social, just as much as for purely physical, reasons: while sexual intimacy plays an undoubted part in their amours, the real driving force in these affairs is that desire for companionship and completeness which only the other sex can give. This is not said to excuse the immoralities of any, but rather to explain the deep nature of that fundamental urge which drives limited and incomplete human beings to each other in an often frantic effort to find wholeness: a wholeness which they can never find alone or with friends of the same sex, however close and intimate. Vain the effort may be when pursued in the wrong way—and if sex be an 'image within an image' it may be called blasphemous as well—but the very heat of the pursuit is a witness to the true pattern of wholeness that is waiting to be found.

For sex is the great *natural* means of wholeness and union. But because a union of persons involves the supernatural as well, or at least is capable of doing so, therefore sex has to be taken up into something far greater if it is to fulfil itself. Natural though its desires and hungers may be, they can only be fulfilled in something greater than the natural. Until men and women learn this, they will continue to let sex destroy them. But the remedy for their ills does not lie in turning against sex, but in finding its true purpose and in seeing how it may be transformed.

It has already been suggested that romantic love was the great *natural* means of coming back to that simpler and more single knowledge which lay behind the Fall of Man. Furthermore, we said that the grand experiment, as worked out in marriage, was the great *natural* means of transforming romantic love into at least the lower reaches of *caritas*. It may be that our use of the word 'natural' has raised difficulties for the orthodox. But we did not suggest that either of these things, and certainly not the second, worked automatically. They were never inevitable results, they were only possibilities. But possibilities they remain, and it is as such that we ought now to be able to see them.

The word which Charles Williams would probably have used is 'inducements'. In that long and rather difficult history of the Christian Church which he called *The Descent of the Dove* he has certain things to say about sex which are worth noting. First of all he suggests that the Primitive Church had a subtler understanding of sex than we have; that they knew of something which later ages have lost or forgotten. He mentions the institution of the *subintroductae*, so ponderously mocked at by Gibbon, and says that there was here a kind of polarisation of sex that was very fruitful. He adds, maddeningly, that we have no knowledge of what this process was, and he himself gives no hints either. But when he comes to the period of the growth of asceticism he makes his great point. There is a reference to the Desert Fathers, those hermits who fled from the world into the desert and who have become the prototypes of all who follow the Way of Rejection. They not only renounced sex, they were obviously terrified of it. Considering what sex was doing in the world, and even within the bounds of the Church, there was some reason for their fear. It is of these Desert Fathers that he says: 'Sex—the poor ignorant creatures thought—was one of the greatest, most subtle, and most lasting of all distractions; nor had the Church . . . shown any striking sign of intending to exhibit it as sometimes the greatest, most splendid, and most authoritative of all inducements.'[1]

[1] *The Descent of the Dove*, p. 56.

Distractions from, or inducement to—what? In the context the distraction can only be from the vision of God. That sex can be a most powerful force dragging anyone away from this is true enough, as the Church has always known. (But need she have stressed it quite so much, and to the almost complete exclusion of other and even worse distractions?) Heath-Stubbs' comment[1] that, according to Williams, every lover is, whether he knows it or not, a religious mystic, shows that he at least believes that the inducement pointed in the same direction. Or at any rate could do so. In so far as sex is inevitably bound up with romantic love, we have shown that this is true. It can be an inducement to the 'first preparatory form' of the vision, anyway; and for innumerable devout and simple lovers it has been so, whether they realised it or not.

It is here that the whole business of the alleged two patterns comes in. There are not two patterns at all; there is only one pattern of glory, whether of Divine Love or of human love. And the pattern is finally the same whether in fact it be followed by the Way of Affirmation or by that of Rejection. (Indeed, every soul must to some extent use both.) But the false knowledge and the divided apprehension, the power and unruliness of natural but improperly controlled desires, have to our eyes split its reflection in two. We divide Divine Love and 'ordinary love', to our great loss and the clouding of our apprehension of the largesse of God and His gifts. In doing this, we have seemed to divide the pattern of love from the pattern of marriage. We should note that nothing

[1] See above, p. 82.

we may have said earlier about either part in isolation
having a real effectiveness of its own within its stunted
limitations, must blind us to the tragedy of this
apparent split. Even if it be hesitantly allowed that
there may be a kind of glory in either separated part,
the glory of the whole pattern is split. And now we
must try to unite the fragments together again. That
is the task of Redemption 'for to make . . . of twain
one new man, so making peace'.[1]

This task of re-uniting love and marriage into the
one true pattern would seem to be particularly relevant
to the present age. We find ourselves living in an age
when two things seem to have happened simultaneously. Marriage as an institution has begun to fail;
romantic love has grown too fast and too quickly.
We are breaking the bonds of the one, but, in doing
so, we are fastening upon ourselves too firmly the
bonds of the other. The result of the breakdown of the
one and the over-admiration of the other, is that
neither marriage nor love can now be seen in proper
focus. Neither of them is seen for what it really is.
The split in the pattern is hiding the glory.

But the important thing to realise is this. Though
romantic love may have got 'loosed on the world' and
may have taken charge in an alarming manner, yet
this discovery of romantic love that has been going on
in our Western world for some centuries is itself a
matter of fundamental value. It seems to have split
the pattern, but it is really the discovery of a part of the
pattern that had not been known before. The split is
at least partly due to an enlargement of our knowledge

[1] Ephesians 2: 15.

of the whole. And it is only by seeing both parts—even if at present we can only see them as wrongly isolated from each other—that we can ever hope one day to see them whole, the full pattern with the glory unbroken. It might well be said that God, in His Divine Providence and largesse, allowed our Western world to make precisely this discovery. We were allowed to do it in order that one day the whole of humanity might see the pattern whole and undivided. It may be our tragedy that we have split it in two and thus dimmed the glory, but the thing itself was surely sent us from that Beatitude to which it can directly lead. To our secularised world which has lost any real conception of Heaven or of the Vision of God, this discovery may perhaps be intended as an 'inducement', a means by which we may come back to an apprehension of these things. It may be given us as the great natural means of recovery. Natural; but not excluding the supernatural. 'First preparatory form' perhaps; but that may be all that modern young people are able to assimilate.

The task of Redemption, and of the Church as the instrument of Redemption, is to re-unite the split reflections of the pattern of love, to show the world the glory which it misunderstands. Thus we are back at the beginning again, for this task will begin only when the real meaning of the vision of romantic love is understood alike by the Church and by the world. If only the world can be made to see the real implications of that disturbing vision which it knows only too well, if once it can see the necessity for fidelity and permanence before the pattern can be worked out, then it may begin to look back with a strange regret to the glories of marriage in an earlier and more stable age. It will certainly find that chopping and changing do not work; they crack the grand experiment too easily.

But the Church has something to learn as well. She must re-discover the fact that in romantic love, re-garded as an ingredient in the Way of Affirmation, she holds one of the greatest inducements to the seeking of true beatitude. She must look at the glories which are shown in some degree by all true lovers.

'Glory'; we have used that word twice, once in each connection. But there is something which only such a word can describe in the way in which Chrètien de Troyes joined both parts of the pattern together as long ago as the twelfth century. He may have been only a lone pioneer, or a voice crying in the wilderness of utilitarian marriage and adulterous romance, but he must have seen the pattern whole when he wrote: 'And Cligès still called his wife mistress and love, and she had no loss of love to complain of, for he loved her always as his lady, and she him as her lover, and every day their love grew stronger.' [1] We can all look back to the age of 'arranged marriages' and see husbands and wives whose lives were a glory as this was. There were of course other homes as well, but, compared with our modern semi-permanent, charge-partners, marriage, there is about many nineteenth-century families a glory which we have utterly lost. And all of us can look around and find very easily the glory of young love caught up in the vision of recognition. Two

[1] *Cligès*; quoted in *Arthurian Torso*, p. 52.

split parts of one pattern? But when the pattern is seen in the glory of its true wholeness, there may perhaps dawn on the world a new kind of marriage altogether. Maybe that is why God is allowing us to be confused.